YOUR PERSONAL DEVOTIONAL LIFE

• • •

A LIFE CHANGING EXPERIENCE

BOBBY MOOR

Scripture quotations are taken from the King James Version.

Scripture quotations marked (NAS) are taken from the New
American Standard Bible, © 1960, 1962, 1963, 1968, 1971, 1972,
1973, 1975, and 1977 by the Lockman Foundation, La Habra, CA.
Used by permission.

Scripture quotations marked (NIV) are taken from the Holy
Bible: New International Version® NIV® Copyright © 1973, 1978,
1984 by International Bible Society. Used by permission of
Zondervan Publishing House. All rights reserved.

Scripture quotations marked (AB) are taken from the
Amplified Bible.

Copyright © The Lockman Foundation 1954, 1958, 1987, Used
by permission.

Song "In The Morning" words and music composed by David
P. Williams, used by permission.

Song "The Quiet Time" words and music by Ron and Patricia
Owens, used by permission.

FIRST EDITION, 2001
SECOND EDITION, 2002
THIRD EDITION, 2004

ISBN 0-9709938-0-3

Printed by

⳨he King's
PRESS

P.O. Box 144
Southaven, MS 38671

DEDICATION

My gratitude to Dr. Stephen Olford, who God used to start and motivate my personal devotional life; to my wife, Joyce, who demonstrates the personal devotional life daily and who encouraged me to spend many hours in my personal devotional life and working on this book; to my secretary, Vicki Taylor, for her untiring assistance in preparing the manuscript for this book and to Mr. Sandy Stroud for his help with the cover layout.

ACKNOWLEDGMENTS

My heart has been challenged afresh with the necessity of a quality personal devotional life as presented by Pastor Bobby Moore. As I read "Your Personal Devotional Life," I found myself longing for more time with the Savior. It caused me to reevaluate my own personal time alone with God. I think this book is one of the best works I have read about personal devotions and intimacy with God. It is very inspiring yet extremely practical. You will be challenged, encouraged, and instructed in the ways of personal time with God. If you have struggled with your time with God, this is the book for you. Dr. Moore will teach you how to have a quality time with God. If you are so busy that you find little time for God, then Pastor Moore will help you reprioritize. If you know what you need to do but just cannot seem to do it, then my friend, Bobby Moore, will come along side you in his book and help you find the strength to spend time with God. Pastor Moore says that time with God changed his Christian life completely. If you read this book prayerfully, I am convinced that God will do in you what he has done in Bobby Moore.

DR. SAMMY TIPPIT

The barometer of the Christian life is the daily, disciplined, and directed communion with the Lord in the light of His Word and the leading of His Spirit. My very dear friend and fellow pastor, Dr. Bobby Moore, has addressed this crucial subject in his new book, "Your Personal Devotional Life." It is biblical, practical, and above all, readable. Its fresh and forthright approach will both challenge and change the serious reader for good and God's glory. I wholeheartedly commend it with a prayer that it will reach multitudes.

DR. STEPHEN F. OLFORD

Bobby Moore is the most qualified of men to write a book on a devotional life. His discipline to time with Christ is without parallel among the thousands of ministers I have known. The result of this close relationship with Jesus is evident in his personal holiness, positive attitude of faith, and the great church and school he has built. But most of all, the results are seen in the fantastic relationship he has with his wife and children. Thank you Brother Bobby for writing a book to show us how you became such a bright, shining light. These pages will transform thousands of discouraged, defeated Christians. This book is a must for every Christian and an appropriate gift for all who are concerned about their family and friends.

DR. MOODY ADAMS

I have never met anyone with a deeper devotional life than Dr. Bobby Moore. His insights can be trusted because they have been forged over decades of daily meetings with God. Every time I fellowship with Brother Bobby, I am drawn one step closer to the One with whom he walks and talks. If you desire to truly commune with God, I cannot imagine a better guide than this practical book.

BRYON PAULUS
Life Action Ministries

The book, "The Devotional Life," is a kaleidoscope of a godly man's journey through the joys, successes, heartaches, and disappointments of life. God has woven into the fabric of Dr. Bobby Moore's life a multicolored glimpse of the glory of God as he has consistently and with confidence learned the secret of being alone with his Creator, Savior, and Lord. You will find the message and teachings of "The Devotional Life" to be very personal, practical and powerful. "The Devotional Life" can be a great tool in your spiritual life as you put its principles into practice.

REV. TONY TRUNNELL
Pastor, Calvary Baptist Church
Bristol, Tennessee

The daily, 24 hour a day, intimate relationship of love with God and His Son, enabled by the Holy Spirit, is the very heart and essence of the Christian's life.

But all too many simply do not know what to do, or how to do it. This book is without question the best book in its clearness and thoroughness I have ever read. For the sincere believer, this is a "must" for their life. I know the author, and that makes this book authentic.

Dr. Henry Blackaby
Henry Blackaby Ministries

The personal relationship with God is the most precious thing in the world. There are few guides that teach you how to practice it. Bobby Moore's book is such a very needed guide. One can profit immensely from practicing what is so methodically taught in this book.

Dr. Josef Tson
President, Romanian Missionary Society

INTRODUCTION

This book is the result of my pilgrimage in the personal devotional life. I do not write as an "expert" on the personal devotional life, but as a learner. The Lord Jesus is teaching me much about Himself and myself through my personal devotional times with Him. My hope is that I can encourage you in your personal devotional life by relating what God is teaching me and how God is changing me. My prayer is that many who read about the personal devotional life will catch the spirit of excitement that God is giving me about this vital part of the Christian life. I am convinced that until we get serious about the personal devotional life, we will never experience the presence and power of the Lord Jesus in an intimate and life-changing manner.

What I hope to accomplish in this book is to help you gain an understanding of the personal devotional life; of the life changing power of the personal devotional life; of the importance of the personal devotional life; of some patterns of the devotional life; of facing and overcoming obstacles and frustrations in the personal devotional life; of the place of prayer and fasting in the personal devotional life; of the place of meditation in the personal devotional life; of the importance of journaling in the personal devotional life; and of the benefits and blessings of the personal devotional life. I want to do more than give information about the personal devotional life. I have a burning desire in my heart that Christians of all ages and cultures would embrace this wonderful, life changing experience of the daily devotional life. No matter who you are or what your circumstances in life may be, the personal devotional life can become for you a thrilling, life changing adventure. I pray that God will spark a fire in your heart that will explode into a lifestyle of daily meeting with God. By developing a personal devotional life with God, you will have the privilege of not only learning about Him, but also spending time with Him.

CONTENTS

YOUR PERSONAL
DEVOTIONAL LIFE

There have been several special life changing experiences in my life. Birth . . . the new Birth . . . God's calling into the ministry . . . marriage . . . children . . . etc. One of the most important life changing experiences of my life took place in the morning service during a Bible Conference at First Evangelical Church in Memphis, Tennessee. Dr. Stephen Olford was the speaker. His sermon was about the Christian's quiet time, titled "Manna in the Morning." That morning God's Spirit confronted me in an area of my life where I was spiritually blind. I was a college and seminary graduate and pastoring a church, but I had never developed a meaningful personal devotional life. I had studied to pass tests in Bible classes and prepared lessons and sermons, but I had failed to establish a personal devotional life where I focused on God and His Word for my personal spiritual worship and development. When Dr. Olford gave the invitation that morning I was the only person who made a public response. At the close of the service, Dr. Olford took me aside and gave me instructions on how to have a personal devotional life. It is difficult to put into words what that day meant to my life. It was the beginning of my daily devotional life. My life has never been the same. I have experienced a fresh and deepening love relationship with God that I did not know could ever be possible.

What mental images does the personal devotional life create in your mind? An indescribable delight? A chore? A sense of frustration? A nagging guilt? Although most Christians realize the need for a daily personal devotional life, many are uneasy, uncertain, and undecided as to how to accomplish the task in a personally satisfying manner.

At a national seminar for Christian workers, a survey

was taken where the question was asked, "What will you be the most ashamed of when you get to Heaven, and what will you wish you would have changed?" The over-whelming response was, "My personal devotional life."

Jerry Vines, pastor of First Baptist Church in Jacksonville, Florida, said about the personal devotional life, "The most important time of the day is early in the morning at my devotional time. I let the Lord speak to me from the Bible, and I speak to the Lord in prayer. That is what keeps me fresh and close to the Lord. It is the sweetest, most precious time in my life."

Charles Stanley, pastor of First Baptist Church in Atlanta, Georgia, states, "The most important activity in the life of any Christian is their private devotions, reading and meditating upon the Word of God and prayer. Your devotional life determines the effectiveness of everything else you are and do." He also said, "The most important thing in my life is an intimate, personal relationship with Jesus Christ. A personal devotional time is focused time spent with God that nurtures that relationship."

> *My quiet time alerts me to what God wants*
> *to do in my life the rest of the day.*

Henry Blackaby, author of **Experiencing God**, says of his devotional life: "My quiet time is not for a devotional thought, but for a deeper relationship with my Heavenly Father. My quiet time alerts me to what God wants to do in my life the rest of the day."

Without question, I believe the most important activity in the life of any Christian is their personal devotional life. Everything in your Christian life rises or falls on your personal devotional life. It is the barometer of your Christian life.

The personal devotional life is more than just a nice idea. No matter who you are — new Christian, old Christian, pastor, or lay person — you have little hope of living victoriously unless you regularly make time to develop a meaningful relationship with God through your personal devotional life. The purpose of the devotional life is to get acquainted with your Heavenly Father, to enjoy His presence, peace, joy, wisdom, strength, forgiveness, guidance, and much more. It will keep you from losing God consciousness.

Jerry Bridges of the Navigators says, "The greatest mistake made in the Christian life is that we rob God of the time He wants to spend with us. I have discovered that I need time each day for feasting on God's Word in parts of Scripture that I am not preaching or teaching from. This helps me keep my personal devotional time from becoming Bible study or preaching and teaching preparation. It allows me to hear from God about me. It's not a time to consider what I think others need to hear, but rather to listen to the Spirit tell me what I need to hear. My devotional time is a time of intimacy with God and a time filled with worship and adoration of God."

> *Love can only be cultivated adequately in aloneness with the One you love.*

In the missionary world, there is no name more revered than that of Hudson Taylor. A remarkable man, Hudson Taylor, was the father of modern faith missions. What was it that made Hudson Taylor the man he became and the man he was right to the end?

His son and daughter-in-law, who traveled constantly with him in his later years, testify that very often they would be traveling over a hard cobblestone road for many hours in a springless cart. Arriving at a Chinese inn late at night, they would endeavor to obtain a little corner of a room for their father. In those inns, there was usually just one large room where everybody slept. Hudson Taylor was now an aged man, but, without fail, every morning just before dawn there would be the scratching of a match and the lighting of a candle, and Hudson Taylor would worship God. This was the key to his life. *It was said that even before the sun rose on China, Hudson Taylor was worshipping God.*

What was the key to Hudson Taylor's life? He loved his Lord and cultivated that love. After all, it is the first commandment. *Love can only be cultivated adequately in aloneness with the one you love, and Hudson Taylor guarded this right to the end.*

Charles Spurgeon writing about the personal devotional life said: "It should be our rule never to see the face of men before first seeing the face of God. The morning watch anchors the soul so that it will not very readily drift far away from God during the day; the morning is the gate of the day and it should be well guarded with prayer. He who rushes from his bed to his business without first spending time with God is as foolish as though he had not washed or dressed, and as unwise as one dashing to battle without arms or armor."

Joseph Carroll writes of A.W. Tozer's devotional life, "I have had the privilege of listening to most of the men who would be considered the great preachers in the world today. One who is now with the Lord is A.W. Tozer. He labored in the city of Chicago for many years. He was different for he spoke with a freshness and with a penetration that was most rare."

When an acquaintance of mine who was called to minister in Chicago arrived in that city, A.W. Tozer called him and said, "This city is a devil's den. It is a very difficult place to minister the Word of God and you will come up against much opposition from the enemy. If you ever want to pray with me, I am at the lakeside every morning at five-thirty. Just make your way down and we can pray together."

Not wanting to bother the great man as he was seeking the Lord, my acquaintance did not immediately accept his offer. *But one day he was so troubled that he made his way very early to the lakeside, about six o'clock, only to find God's servant prostrate upon the sand worshipping God.* Needless to say, he did not disturb him.

A.W. Tozer worshipped God daily in his personal devotional life. He was one of the few men who taught and preached consistently on the need of the personal devotional life, conveying in no uncertain manner that personal worship was the missing jewel among Christians.

John Maxwell said of his personal devotional life, "I would say 90% of my spiritual leadership growth has been a result of my quiet time with God. In that time, God comforts me, provides ideas, wisdom, and reveals His will.

Most importantly, my prayer time is where I get to know God better and enjoy spiritual intimacy with the Father."

David Manley, who is the president of our Christian school, says that his ability to lead effectively is dependent upon the time he spends with God in his personal devotional life.

Following a preaching service in Hagerstown, Maryland, my wife and I were listening to an interview program on a Christian radio station originating from the Moody Radio network. The son of one of the leading preachers in America was being interviewed. His father preached yearly in some of the great churches of our land. Tragically, this talented and heralded preacher chose a life of secret sin that caused his downfall and death. In the interview, the preacher's son was asked the question, "Could you tell when your dad began to fall spiritually?" He replied, "When my dad stopped reading his Bible devotionally, he began to fall spiritually." As I listened to this radio program and the tragic failure of this man of God, I could not get away from this thought: "How many Christians have never started reading their Bibles devotionally?"

The success or failure of your Christian life, ministry, and witness can hinge on your personal devotional life. When people do not have a consistent personal devotional life, they begin to self-destruct. There is only one way any of us can grow and be upheld in our walk with the Lord, and that is through daily communion with our Lord and His Word and prayer.

WHAT IS THE PERSONAL

DEVOTIONAL LIFE?

The purpose of the personal devotional life is to meet God . . . to experience God . . . to worship God . . . to commune with God. It is a time of personal fellowship with God. It is when God speaks to me about Himself, His will, and His working in my life. It is a time of giving my life, family, and concerns to God on a daily basis. With all the pressures of work, home, ministry, etc., personal meetings with God often are neglected. The personal devotional life enables you to meet with God every day to celebrate who He is and who you are in Christ, to connect and commune with God in His Word and in prayer, to listen to His counsel and direction, to chronicle the activities of God in your life, to commit your life, family, church, cares and day to the Lord, and to clothe yourself in the whole armor of God.

The personal devotional life is called by many, the Christian's quiet time. It is the time set aside each day for prayer, Scripture reading, meditation, personalizing the Scripture and the cultivation of the spiritual life. The devotional life is a focused time spent with God that nurtures your personal relationship with the Lord Jesus Christ. The personal devotional life consists of those priority moments of each day when the Christian experiences personal worship and communion with his Lord. It is that time when the believer listens to the voice of His Heavenly Father from the Bible and communes with Him in prayer. It is a daily time for nourishing your spiritual life through talking with God and feeding upon His Word. Warren Wiersbe defines the personal devotional life as meeting with God everyday in His Word, in prayer, and in worship.

The basis for the devotional life is time for God and time with God. It is a time devoted to a person, that person being the Lord Jesus Christ. Joseph Parker said, "Every morning the soul should come into conscious contact with God, if only for a few moments — the very touch will invigorate and cheer the life, and call forth the truest sensitiveness of the moral nature."

Rex Holt, pastor of the Baptist Temple in McAllen, Texas, says, "The purpose of the devotional life is reading God's Word, listening to Him speak and bringing my life under His care and control." A little boy who entered his father's office best illustrates the purpose of the devotional time. When his father asked what he wanted, the little boy replied, "Oh nothing; I just wanted to be with you." Steve Wilkes, a member of my congregation and Professor of Evangelism and Missions at Mid-America Baptist Theological Seminary, shares that the purpose of the devotional time is simply to establish and maintain a daily, personal walk with the Lord Jesus Christ.

Patrick Morley says: "The personal devotional life or quiet time is a routine period, usually at the beginning or end of the day, in which five, ten, fifteen, thirty minutes, an hour or more are set aside to read and study God's Word, pray and possibly perform other spiritual disciplines."

> *The purpose of the personal devotional life is to meet God . . . to experience God . . . to worship God . . . to commune with God.*

Ron and Patricia Owens wrote a song about the quiet time that clearly defines the meaning of the personal devotional life:

The Quiet Time

Ron and Patricia Owens

The quiet time, the quiet time when I sit at Jesus' feet,
Those special hallowed moments when the earth and heaven
meet.
Preparing for the day ahead, I feast upon the Living Bread.
My soul's restored, my heart's renewed in the quiet time.

The quiet time, the quiet time, the Spirit's voice I hear,
Communing with my blessed Lord, His holy presence near.
I look into His matchless face, I praise Him for His amazing
grace,
I face the day, I go with Him from the quiet time.

The Scripture is filled with examples of those who had a personal devotional life. Abraham is the first person in the Scripture to demonstrate a personal devotional life. Genesis 19:27 states of Abraham, "He got up early in the morning to the place where he stood before the Lord." Genesis 22:3 says, "Abraham rose up early in the morning . . . and went into the place of which God had told him." These verses emphasize the personal accountability, privilege, priority, obedience and private worship of the believer with God. He met the Lord early in the morning. He met the Lord in a specific place. He met the Lord.

Jacob, in Genesis 28:18-22, gives us another example of the personal devotional life. The Scripture says of him, "And Jacob rose up early in the morning, and took the stone that he had put for his pillow, and set it up for a pillar, and poured oil on the top of it. And he called the name of that place Bethel: but the name of that city was called Luz at first. And Jacob vowed a vow, saying, 'If God will be with me, and will keep me in this way that I go, and will give me bread to eat, and raiment to put on, so that I come again to my father's house in peace; then shall the Lord be my God: And this stone, which I have set for a pillar, shall be God's house: and of all that Thou shalt give me I will surely give the tenth unto Thee.'" Jacob's commitment to God is the outstanding feature of his personal devotional life. The personal devotional time is a time of surrender and commitment to the Lord. Notice that Jacob, like Abraham, met the Lord early in the morning.

Moses gives us another example of the personal devotional life. In Exodus 34:2, the Scripture says, "Be ready in the morning, and come up in the morning unto Mount Sinai, and present yourself there unto me on the top of the mountain" (NAS). Moses' personal devotional life was marked by his personal choice to worship the Lord and his seeking the Lord's guidance in his life and the life of the people of God.

Exodus 34 is an example of Moses' personal devotional life. Note the elements in his personal time with the Lord.

1. His preparation "be **ready** in the morning" — vs. 2.
2. He presented himself to the Lord "present **yourself** there to me" — vs. 2.
3. His meeting with God was personal and private "**no man** shall come up with thee" — vs. 3.
4. He experienced the presence of God "**the Lord descended** in the cloud and **stood with him** there" — vs. 5.
5. He worshipped the Lord "Moses made haste, and bowed his heart toward the earth, and **worshipped**" —vs. 8.
6. He interceded for his people "O Lord, let my Lord, I pray thee, go among us; for it is a stiff-necked people; and **pardon our iniquity** and our sin, and take us for Thine inheritance" — vs. 9.
7. God gave him instructions and directions for himself and his people — vs. 10-28.
8. He was transformed through his meeting with God "the children of Israel saw **the face of Moses**, that the skin of Moses' face shone" — vs. 34.
9. He shared with others what God had shared with him "**And Moses called unto them**; and Aaron and all the rulers of the congregation returned unto him; and Moses talked with them. And gave them **a commandment all that the Lord had spoken with him** in Mount Sinai" — vs. 31,32.
10. He chronicled — journalized God's activity in his

life "the Lord said to Moses, **write thou these words**; for after the terror of these words I have made a covenant with thee and with Israel" — vs. 27.

The devotional life of David is described in Psalm 5:3, "Morning by morning, O Lord, You hear my voice, morning by morning I lay my requests before Thee and wait in expectation" (NIV). David's devotional life was characterized by communing with God, asking requests of God, and waiting in expectation on God. II Samuel 7:18-29 records one of David's devotional times.

1. He sat before the Lord gaining perspective on what he should do (vs. 18).
2. Reviewing the past blessings of God (vs. 18-21).
3. Reflecting on the nature of God (vs. 22-24).
4. Remembering the promises of God (vs. 25-28).
5. He made request of God (vs. 29).

The prophet Isaiah describes the devotional life with these words, "The Lord God hath given me the tongue of the learned (a disciple), that I should know how to speak a word in season to him who is weary, He awakeneth morning by morning; He awaketh mine ear to hear like the learned (a disciple). The Lord God hath opened mine ear, and I was not rebellious, neither turned backward" (Isaiah 50:4,5). This passage reveals several aspects of the devotional life. They are hearing from God, communing with God, and obeying God on a daily basis.

Daniel was the Prime Minister of a great empire. He was undoubtedly much busier than you and me. If anyone could have said, "I don't have time to meet with God daily," it was Daniel. Yet he met with God three times daily. Daniel 6:10 says, "Three times a day he got down on his knees and prayed, giving thanks to his God" (NIV). Conviction, commitment and communion with God characterized his devotional life.

Ezekiel described the devotional life as, "In the morning came the Word of the Lord unto me" (Ezekiel 12:8). His devotional life majored on hearing from God on a daily basis.

> *Our Lord never missed His quiet time.*

The devotional life of the Lord Jesus Christ is described in Mark 1:35, "And in the morning, rising up a great while before day, He went out, and departed into a solitary place, and there prayed." The reference in Isaiah 50:4-5 refers to the devotional life of the Lord Jesus Christ. Dr. Stephen Olford points out several things about our Lord's devotional life. There was devotional openness. "Morning by morning He awakens (opens) my ear (vs. 4)." Our Lord never missed His quiet time. Every morning He was open to the voice of His Father. His daily request was, "Speak, Lord, thy servant heareth."

There was devotional obedience. "The Lord God has opened my ear, and I was not rebellious, neither turned backward (vs. 5)." Our Lord obeyed instantly and completely what the Father said to Him.

There was devotional overflow. "The Lord God hath given me the tongue of the learned (a disciple), that I should know how to speak a word in season to him that is weary (vs. 4)." The natural overflow of the devotional life is the ability to speak a word in season to needy men and women around us.

In the Old Testament, the Levites stood "every morning to thank and praise the Lord, and likewise at evening" (I Chronicles 23:30). According to the New Testament, all believers are priests (I Peter 2:5,9). The personal devotional life is the privilege and priority of every believer in Christ.

> *Church history is replete with examples of those who practiced a devotional life.*

Alexander Maclaren, one of the great Biblical expositors, declared that he owed all that was in himself and his ministry to the habit, never broken, of spending one hour a day "alone with the Eternal." The hour, which he took, was from nine to ten in the morning. His assistant said he was sometimes allowed to be in the room with him but no word was passed between them. In his well-worn armchair he sat, with the big Bible on his knees, sometimes reading its pages, more frequently his hand over his face. During that hour he did not allow himself to read even the Bible for texts, or as a student. It was read as a child would read a letter from an absent father, as a loving heart would drink in again the message from a loved one far away.

Martin Luther, one of the leaders in the Protestant reformation, had a very vital and strong devotional life. He said he could not survive spiritually without three hours a day in prayer and the Word. A Christian's spiritual fitness requires daily fresh encounters with God in the Scripture and in prayer.

> *God does nothing but in answer to prayer.*

John Wesley, the founder of the Methodist church, said, "God does nothing but in answer to prayer." He backed up his conviction by devoting two hours daily to the sacred exercise of prayer and the devotional reading of God's Word. One of the great things we learn from John Wesley about the devotional life is that it is a discipline that brings delight and never drudgery.

The most notable feature of David Brainerd's life and ministry to the Indians of North America was his personal devotional life, prayer, fasting and meditation on God's Word. Brainerd said, "I love to be alone in my cottage, where I can spend much time in prayer and in God's Word."

Adoniram Judson, missionary pioneer to Burma, sought to withdraw from business and company seven times a day in order to engage in the devotional study of God's Word and prayer.

It is said of George Whitefield, the mighty preacher during America's second great awakening, that the grand secret of his power was his devotional life. Had he been less prayerful, he would have been less powerful. His diary shows his unyielding adherence to his "stated hours of prayer;" first thing in the morning, again at noon, and finally at night. His devotional and study times found him on his knees with his English Bible, his Greek Testament, and Matthew Henry's Commentary spread out before him. It was his practice to pray over every line and word of both the English and Greek till the passage, in its essential message, had veritably become part of his own soul.

The English preacher Joseph Parker said, "The morning is the time for meeting the Lord, for then we are at our best, having a new supply of energy. Blessed is the day that is opened with prayer! Holy is the dawn that finds us on 'top of the mount' with God!"

Bishop Taylor Smith of the Anglican Church, was known as the "Quiet Time man." He devoted his early morning hours to pouring over God's Word and then pouring out his heart to God in prayer.

Graham Scroggie, a great Bible teacher of the twentieth century, states: "Early in the morning, after having asked in a few words the Lord's blessings upon His precious Word, I begin to meditate upon the Word of God, searching for the sake of obtaining food for my own soul."

The powerful ministry of Charles Simeon, covering a fifty-four year pastorate in Cambridge, England was attributed to his personal devotional life. His friend, R. Housman, stayed with him for a few months and tells us something of this man's devotion: "Never did I see such consistency, and reality of devotion, such warmth of piety, such zeal and love . . . Invariably he arose every morning, though it was the winter season, at four o'clock; and after lighting his fire, he devoted the first four hours of the day to private prayer and the devotional study of the Scriptures . . . Here was the secret of his great grace and spiritual strength. Deriving instruction from such a source, and seeking it with such diligence, he was comforted in all his trials and prepared for every duty."

Lt. General William K. Harrison was the most decorated soldier in the 30th Infantry Division, rated by General Eisenhower as the number one infantry division in World War II. General Harrison was the first American to enter Belgium during the war, which he did at the head of the Allied forces. He received every decoration for valor except the Congressional Medal of Honor — being honored with the Distinguished Service Cross, the Silver Star, the Bronze Star for Valor, and the Purple Heart. When the Korean War began, he served as Chief of Staff in the United Nations Command and because of his character and calm self-control was ultimately President Eisenhower's choice to head the long and tedious negotiations to end the war.

General Harrison was a soldier's soldier who led a busy, ultra-kinetic life, but he was also an amazing man of the Word. When he was a twenty-year-old West Point cadet, he began reading the Old Testament through once and the New Testament four times annually. General Harrison did this until the end of his life. Even in the thick of war he maintained his commitment by catching up during the two- and three-day respites for replacement and refitting that followed battles, so that when the war ended he was right on schedule. When at the age of ninety his failing eyesight no longer permitted this discipline, he had read the Old Testament seventy times and the New Testament 280 times! No wonder his godliness and wisdom were proverbial. It is no surprise that the Lord used him for eighteen fruitful years to lead Officers Christian Fellowship.

General Harrison's story tells us that it is possible, even for the busiest of us, to systematically train ourselves in God's Word. His life also remains a demonstration of the benefits of a godly mind's programming itself with Scripture. His closest associates say that every area of his life (domestic, spiritual, and professional) and each of the great problems he faced was informed by the Scriptures. People marveled at his godliness and his ability to bring the Word's light to every area of life.

What do you think about when you first wake up? Why not follow the practice of these great men of God, who met God in His Word and directed their prayer to God in the morning and looked to Him for strength? It is important to begin each day with Jesus.

But God does not expect an exemplary and exciting

personal devotional life from only some of the great saints of history. He desires that ordinary Christians like you and me commit ourselves to a personal devotional life and develop that devotional lifestyle into the very heart and soul of our Christian life.

God has greatly used a layman in my church to demonstrate the value and power of the personal devotional life. In a Prayer Conference in our church in 1996, God moved on the heart of one of our laymen, Jerry Cherry, to establish a Prayer Partner's Ministry. God has led Jerry to dedicate the early morning hours to prayer and to God's Word. God has used this daily devotional time to change his life, his marriage, his family, his friends, his business, his church, his pastor, and other churches and pastors. God will do the same for any lay person or minister who will establish a consistent devotional life.

WHAT DOES IT MEAN TO READ THE BIBLE DEVOTIONALLY?

One of the essential ingredients in the personal devotional life is reading God's Word devotionally. What does it mean to read the Bible devotionally? After preaching a message in which I frequently used the term "the personal devotional life," a man approached me and asked, "What do you mean by the personal devotional life and reading your Bible devotionally?" After years of having a personal devotional life, God has led me to approach the reading of His Word in the following manner. It will explain what I mean by the personal devotional life.

> *God whispered words in my spirit I will never forget. He said, "This Bible is my personal letter to you."*

1. *Read God's Word as a personal letter from God.* Do not let your reading of God's Word be theoretical. Make it practical. The Bible is filled with examples of the personal aspect of God's Word. Nathan said, "The Word of the Lord came to me" (I Chronicles 17:3). David's last prophetic words were, "The Spirit of the Lord spoke to me" (II Samuel 23:2). Jeremiah said, "The Word of the Lord came to me" (Jeremiah 1:4). God said to and through the apostle John, "These things have I written unto you that believe on the name of the Son of God, that you may know that you have eternal life" (I John 5:13).

When my dear friend Billy Morgan was a missionary in Brazil, he wrote me faithfully. His letters were always personal and interesting. One day after reading a letter from him I picked up my Bible to read it. Regrettably, the letter from Billy Morgan seemed more interesting than the Bible. I immediately confessed to the Lord that my response was wrong. God whispered in my spirit words I will never forget. He said, "This Bible is my personal letter to you." Since that day I have regarded the Bible as God's personal letter to me. It has made a major difference in my life.

Some years ago, a beautiful and single young lady was given a book as a gift. She began to read it, felt it was rather dry and dull, and accordingly put it away in her bookcase. Some time later she was attending a social function when she was introduced to a very charming young man, the center of attraction at the gathering. His name, she learned, was H.W. Wood. During the course of the conversation she said: "Oh, Mr. Wood, I have a book at home written by someone called Wood; in fact, the author has the same initials as you. Isn't that a coincidence?"

"Not at all," was the reply of the young bachelor, "I wrote that book."

When the young lady returned home, she sought out the book and stayed up until after midnight to finish it! Because she had been captivated by the author, she had a sudden desire to read his book, and this time she found it to be most interesting. Later the young lady became Mrs. H.W. Wood! What made a difference? Quite simply: she had come to know the author of the book.

A.W. Tozer said of the personal nature of the Bible, "The Bible is the only living book in the history of the world. It lives because it is the active voice of the living God, communicating Himself to us, His power, His character, His ways of dealing with people. His purposes all remain eternally unchanged and unchanging, revealed in His Word." He further stated, "I think a new world will arise out of the religious mists when we approach our Bible with the idea that it is not only a Book which was once spoken, but a Book which is now speaking."

2. **Read God's Word prayerfully.** Approach the Word of God with the spirit and attitude of David. His spirit and attitude are best demonstrated in his prayers to God. He prayed in Psalm 25:4-5, "Show me thy ways, O Lord; teach me thy paths. Lead me in thy truth, and teach me." In Psalm 119:18 he prayed, "Open my eyes that I may behold wondrous things out of Thy law." When I meet God in my devotional times I pray the promise of God

recorded in James 1:5, "If any of you lack wisdom let him ask of God." I also ask the Lord to do for me what He did for the disciples on the road to Emmaus, "Did not our hearts burn within us, while He talked with us along the way, and while He opened to us the Scriptures" (Luke 24:32).

3. *Read God's Word eagerly and expectantly.* God's counsel to us is "be swift to hear" (James 1:19). The word *"swift"* implies eagerness, intense interest, expectation, and anticipation. The Amplified Bible translates it, "be a ready listener." The New International Version translates it, "quick to listen."

Ezra, the Old Testament leader, demonstrated this quality in his life. The Scripture says of him, "He was a ready scribe in the law of Moses" (Ezra 7:6).

Reading God's Word devotionally involves faith, confidence, and expectancy. This is made clear in Hebrews 11:6, "But without faith it is impossible to please Him; for he that cometh to God must believe that He is, and that He is the rewarder of them that diligently seek Him."

I Peter 2:2, in the Amplified Bible, highlights this spirit of expectancy. It says, "Like newborn babies you should crave — thirst for, earnestly desire the pure (unadulterated) spiritual milk."

4. *Read God's Word humbly with meekness and holiness.* There is a moral qualification for experiencing God in His Word. James 1:21 says, "Wherefore, put away all filthiness and superfluity of naughtiness, and receive with meekness the engrafted Word." The New International Version translates this verse, "Put away all moral filth and the evil that is so prevalent and humbly accept the Word of God." Psalm 24:3-5 clearly gives the conditions for experiencing God, "Who shall ascend into the hill of the Lord? Or who shall stand in His holy place? He who hath clean hands, and a pure heart, who hath not lifted up his soul unto vanity, nor sworn deceitfully. He shall receive the blessing from the Lord, and righteousness from the God of his salvation."

> *Meekness is a combination of humility*
> *and a teachable spirit.*

The latter part of James 1:21 informs us to "receive with meekness the engrafted Word." Meekness is an attitude that accepts and receives God's Word and will without questioning, disputing, and resistance. Meekness is a combination of humility and a teachable spirit. I Peter 2:1 teaches that a holy life is an essential qualification for receiving, personalizing and living according to God's Word. God's Word instructs us to lay aside all malice (every trace of wickedness) AB . . . all guile (deceit), NIV. . . hypocrisies (insincerity and pretense) AB . . . envies (self-centeredness; grudges), AB . . . evil speaking (slander and evil speaking of every kind). These attitudes, actions, and reactions must be laid aside if we are to meet the Lord devotionally in His Word.

5. *Read God's Word carefully and seriously.* There is a particular group of people mentioned in the Bible who were very careful and serious about reading and searching God's Word. They lived in Berea. The Bible says about them, "These were more noble than those in Thessalonica in that they received the Word with all readiness of mind and searched the Scriptures daily." (Acts 17:11). I was asked on one occasion if I regarded and interpreted the Scriptures literally or symbolically. My reply was, "I take the Scriptures seriously." Reading God's Word devotionally implies a sacred and serious approach that involves the personalizing of His Word in our lives.

6. *Read God's Word consistently.* The Bible records that the first century Christians "continued steadfastly in the apostles doctrine" (Acts 2:42). The apostles' doctrine was Biblical teaching from the Old Testament and the teachings of Jesus. The apostle Paul instructed Timothy to "give attendance to reading, to exhortation, and to doctrine" (I Timothy 4:13). This was his way of telling Timothy to stay in the Word of God. Paul also told him to "take heed to thyself and thy doctrine, continue

in them" (I Timothy 4:16). In Second Timothy, he further instructed Timothy to "study to show yourself approved unto God, a workman that needeth not to be ashamed, rightly dividing the word of truth" (II Timothy 2:15). The word "study" implies a continual searching of God's Word with a teachable spirit. James 1:25 instructs us to continue in the devotional reading of the Word of God.

7. *Read God's Word dependently.* The Holy Spirit is the only One who can reveal to us the true meaning and application of Scripture. There must be an absolute dependence upon Him to reveal and teach us the meaning of Scripture. Paul makes this very clear in I Corinthians 2:9-13: "But as it is written, eye hath not seen, nor ear heard, neither have entered into the heart of man, the things which God hath prepared for them that love Him. But God hath revealed them unto us by His Spirit, for the Spirit searcheth all things, yea, the deep things of God. For what man knoweth the things of a man except the spirit of man which is in him? Even so the things of God knoweth no man, but the Spirit of God. Now we have received, not the spirit of the world, but the Spirit who is of God; that we might know the things that are freely given to us of God. Which things also we speak, not in the words which man's wisdom teacheth, but which the Holy Spirit teacheth, comparing spiritual things with spiritual."

> *The Holy Spirit is the only one who can reveal to us the true meaning and application of Scripture.*

Jesus spoke of the Holy Spirit's ministry to us when He said, "When the Comforter is come, He will teach you all things" (John 14:26). He also said, "The Spirit of truth will guide you into all truth" (John 16:13).

8. *Read God's Word obediently.* I heard Peter Lord make a statement that is very important and relative to the Christian life. He said, "It is imperative that the Bible be obeyed as well as interpreted." John 2:5 is an all inclusive word about obedience: "Whatever He saith to you, do it." Jesus said, "If you know these things, happy are you if you do them" (John 13:17). The apostle James

warns us to "be doers of the Word and not hearers only" (James 1:22). God has challenged and changed my life with two verses about obedience: "The Word preached did not profit them, not being mixed with faith" (obedience) (Hebrews 4:2), and "You have purified your souls in obeying the truth through the Spirit unto unfeigned love of the brethren, see that ye love one another with a pure heart fervently" (I Peter 1:22).

These eight insights, into what it means to read the Bible devotionally have enabled me to personalize and live my life according to God's Word. I believe this is what Jesus had in mind when He said, "Man shall not live by bread alone, but by every word that proceedeth out of the mouth of God" (Matthew 4:4).

GOD CAN CHANGE YOU THROUGH YOUR PERSONAL DEVOTIONAL LIFE

Beginning and continuing my personal devotional time with the Lord has been and continues to be a life changing experience for me. My priorities have changed. Meeting with the Lord every morning has become the number one priority of my spiritual life. Looking at my daily devotional life as a personal appointment time with the Lord motivates me to be faithful and consistent in my daily devotional life. I am learning what Andrew Murray meant when he said, "God needs time with us." It is extremely helpful to picture yourself meeting with the Lord Jesus every morning.

> *I discovered that I allowed the urgent to take the place of the most important in my life.*

I have been forced to examine, evaluate, and readjust my priorities in life. The daily priority of most people is preparation for the work day or the school day which includes showering, selecting clothes for the day, breakfast and perhaps the morning paper or the morning news on TV. I discovered that I had allowed the urgent to take the place of the most important in my life.

As I began to have a consistent daily devotional time with the Lord I discovered the power of Jesus words, "Man shall not live by bread alone, but by every word that proceeds out of the mouth of God" (Matthew 4:4). The words of Job have also challenged and changed my priorities, "I have esteemed the words of His mouth more than my necessary food" (Job 23:12).

Because of my daily devotional life, the Lord Himself has become my priority. Seeking Him has become a priority, as Matthew 6:33 says, "Seek ye first the kingdom of God and His righteousness." Loving Him has become a priority as Matthew 22:37 says, "Thou shall love the Lord, thy God, with all thy heart, and with all thy soul, and with all thy mind." Worshipping Him has become a priority as Psalm 118:28 says, "Thou art my God, and I will praise Thee; thou art my God, I will exalt Thee."

My New Testament professor in seminary, Dr. Curtis Vaughan, helped me tremendously when he translated John 1:15 during a study of John's gospel. He translated the statement "He that cometh after me is preferred before me; for He was before me" in this manner. "He, Jesus, who is coming after me is more important than me; He existed before me, and He was my first."

The object of the personal devotional life is a more personal and intimate relationship with God. This is the priority of every believer in Christ. My daily personal devotional life has become a major priority in my life and through my devotional times with God my priorities in life have changed.

My perspective in life and of the Lord changed. The Lord has become near, real, intimate, adequate and awesome. My perspective on problems and people has changed. I began to see them from God's eternal perspective.

As I met with God in my devotional time, several things happened. I began to realize who I am in Christ. I saw myself as God sees me: a saint, a servant, a soldier, a secure one in Christ, one having the strength of Christ and one whose sufficiency and satisfaction was in Christ. I realized that God was at work in my life.

> *I saw that as I ministered and served others I was in reality ministering to and serving Christ.*

My perspective toward others changed. I began to see others through the eyes of God. I saw people as the objects of God's love and care. I saw how God used all kinds of people in my life to conform me to Christ likeness. I saw that as I ministered and served others I was in reality ministering to and serving Christ.

My perspective toward circumstances in life changed. God used Romans 8:28,29 in my life, "And we know that all things work together for good to them that love God, to them who are called according to His purpose. For whom He did foreknow, He also did predestinate to be conformed to the image of His Son." One day God revealed to me that circumstance was His stance and disappointments were His appointments. He also used Philippians 1:12, "But I would you should understand, brethren, that the things which happened unto me have fallen out rather unto the furtherance of the gospel." God gradually showed me that He was developing a life message in me through the happenings of my life in order that I could share and communicate His gospel with others.

He used I Thessalonians 5:18, "In everything give thanks for this is the will of God in Christ Jesus concerning you." God's Spirit convicted me of the sin of ingratitude and thanklessness. In my devotional times with the Lord, He began to change me from a person who took things for granted to a person of gratitude. God changed my response of bitterness to blessing when I began to thank Him for people, pressures and even problems He allowed in my life.

> *Even the "bad things" in life can be good if we see God at work in them.*

God used the testimony of Joseph in Genesis 50:20, "But as for you, you thought evil against me; but God meant it unto good, to bring to pass, as it is this day, to save many people alive." God showed me in my devotional times with Him that He could take the worst possible things in life and turn them into the greatest blessings of life. I started to see that even the "bad things" in life can be good if we see God at work in them.

God also used II Corinthians 3:18 to change my perspective on life and on the Lord. In this verse of Scripture Paul states, "But we all, with unveiled face beholding as in a mirror the glory of the Lord, are changed into the same image from glory to glory, even as by the Spirit of the Lord." God is in the process of changing my life as I meet Him daily in my personal devotional life. As I see Christ in all His glory, He changes me into His likeness.

As God is changing my perspective on life and about Him, the Holy Spirit has developed three convictions that are making a difference in my life: First, to see every person and circumstance through the eyes of God; Second, to evaluate every opportunity and problem on the basis of God's power and ability; Third, to confront every decision, difficulty, and opportunity from the perspective of God's Word, God's Spirit, God's Son and with prayer.

In my daily devotional life with the Lord, writing down the personal things He shows me in His Word gives me a fresh insight into the character and ways of God. I sensed that God was working in my life and that He was interested in every circumstance of my life. In my daily times with Him, He gives me His directions for my day. His presence through the Word and in times of prayer becomes precious to me. I thank God that He is changing me. He can change your entire outlook on life through a consistent personal devotional life.

My personality has changed. Spending time with Jesus every morning changed my character. The person He created me to be began to function as He intended. I am becoming a "new creature in Christ" as II Corinthians 5:17 promises, "Therefore, if any man be in Christ, he is a new creation; old things are passed away; behold, all things are become new." Insecure, unstable, irritable, independent, undisciplined and selfish were words that described my personality prior to starting my personal devotional life. Slowly but surely, the Holy Spirit began to transform my personality from a "flesh driven" Christian to a "Spirit controlled" Christian. A different person, a fully devoted follower of the Lord Jesus Christ is being developed in my daily devotional times with the Lord.

My purpose in life has changed. As I spend time daily with the Lord in His Word and prayer, He has given me seven specific purposes in my life. These purposes have served as God given goals and guidelines in my life. These purposes are:

1. To know and love the Lord (Philippians 3:8,10; Matthew 22:37,38).
2. To live my life under the authority of God's Word (Matthew 4:4; Luke 1:38; Psalm 119:105,128,133; Job 23:12; II Timothy 3:15-17).
3. To live for God's glory (Jeremiah 9:23-24; Malachi 2:1-2; I Corinthians 10:13; II Thessalonians 1:12).
4. To live to become like Christ (Romans 8:28-29; Galatians 4:19; Ephesians 4:13,15; Philippians 1:20-21; 3:10; Colossians 1:28).
5. To live to fulfill the Great Commission (Matthew 28:18-20; Philippians 1:12; I Corinthians 9:19-23).
6. To live as a servant (Matthew 20:26,28; Mark 10:42-45; Luke 16:2; 22:24-27; Galatians 5:13; 6:2; II Corinthians 4:5; II Timothy 2:2).
7. To live to experience revival and become an instrument for revival (Psalm 60:1; 85:6; 138:7; Lamentations 5:21; Hosea 10:12; Habakkuk 3:2; Isaiah 57:15; Acts 3:19).

What God has done in my life, He will do for you! A.W. Tozer said, "Anything that God has ever done, He can do now. Anything that God has done anywhere else, He can do here. Anything that God has done for anyone else, He can do for you."

One of the greatest influences on my personal devotional life came from my wife's mother, Mrs. George Henry. She died recently at the age of 93. During the last years of her life, she developed Alzheimer's disease. Her memory was severely affected by this terrible disease. There were times when she did not know her family. In spite of Alzheimer's disease she maintained her early morning Bible reading and prayer time. Every morning she would read her Bible out loud for an hour. Then she would pray aloud for an hour. In the setting of the prayer time, I heard her pray clearly, consistently and intellectually for her children, their spouses, her grandchildren, missionaries, and her pastor, all of these by name. Her personal devotional life was a source of conviction and encouragement to me. On one occasion she said to me, "My memory is not as good as it once was, but there is one thing I have not forgotten, that I belong to Jesus."

If an aging adult with Alzheimer's can have a daily devotional life, anyone can. It will change your life like it changed my wife's mother.

Think what could happen if every Christian really took his devotional life seriously and began to have a daily time of devotion with God in His Word and prayer. God would be pleased. You would be strengthened and progressively sanctified. The church would become a mighty army of believers. Are you having daily devotional experiences with the Lord? If you are not, will you right this moment, commit yourself to a daily devotional experience with your Lord? You will never regret making this decision. It will bless and benefit you throughout all your life. If you are inconsistent in your daily devotional life, will you recommit yourself to meet with the Lord daily in a vital and life changing devotional time?

THE IMPORTANCE OF

YOUR DEVOTIONAL LIFE

I trusted Christ as my personal Lord and Savior when I was nineteen years of age. I graduated from college and seminary in pursuing preparation for the Gospel ministry. I lived as a Christian and pastored churches during the early years of ministry, but I was not aware of the need for a personal devotional time with the Lord. I studied the Bible, I prepared sermons, I taught and preached, but the devotional dimension of Bible study, prayer and communion with the Lord was missing in my life. As I reflect on forty-five years of Christian ministry, I shudder to think how many pastors, deacons, church leaders and church members — like me — failed to establish a dynamic and consistent personal devotional life.

> *My personal devotional life is, without question, the most important and essential aspect of my Christian life.*

I shall forever be grateful to Dr. Stephen Olford for sharing the message on the Christian quiet time in a Christian Life conference. His message has been published under the title *"Manna in the Morning."* I would encourage every Christian to secure a copy of *"Manna in the Morning"* and use it as a guide to start and develop your devotional life. God used Dr. Olford and his message to challenge me, change me, motivate me, and instruct me in establishing my personal devotional life.

The daily devotional life with God in the Word and prayer should be an experience to enjoy and not an event to endure. In my Christian pilgrimage, God has shown me that my personal devotional life is, without question, the most important and essential aspect of my Christian life.

The daily devotional life is essential to **spiritual growth.** A basic ingredient for spiritual growth is personal time alone with God. It means giving God your undivided attention for a period of time when you talk with God and hear from Him. It is a discipline that will keep your life from becoming stale and stagnant spiritually, and positively, will cause you to grow in spiritual maturity. According to Acts 20:32, it is "the Word of His grace which is able to build you up and give you an inheritance among those who are sanctified."

The psalmist David in Psalm 119:28 prayed to the Lord, "Strengthen me according to Thy Word" (NAS). Job, in the midst of his troubles said, "I have treasured the words of His mouth more than my necessary food" (Job 23:12, NAS).

> *Spiritual growth is an increasing*
> *dependence upon God.*

Simon Peter, under the direction of the Holy Spirit, gave this word of instruction and direction to the Christians of his day. He said, "Like newborn babies, crave pure spiritual milk, so that by it you may grow up" (I Peter 2:2, NIV).

A.W. Tozer in *"The Root of Righteous"* says, "Progress in the Christian life is exactly equal to the growing knowledge we gain of the Triune God in personal experience." And such experience requires a whole life devoted to it and plenty of time spent at the holy task of cultivating God. God can be known satisfactorily only as we devote time to Him. "Have a Little Talk with Jesus," we sing, and we title our books "God's Minute" or something else as revealing. The Christian who is satisfied to give God His "minute" and to have "a little talk with Jesus" is the same one who shows up at the evangelistic service weeping over his retarded spiritual growth and begging the evangelist to show him the way out of his difficulty.

F.B. Meyer said, "All sermons and addresses, all group Bible readings and classes, all religious magazines and books can never take the place of our own quiet study of God's Word. We measure our growth in grace by the growth of our love for private Bible Study."

A thousand distractions would woo us away from thoughts of God, but if we are wise we will sternly put them from us and make room for the King and take time to entertain Him. Some things may be neglected with but little loss to the spiritual life, but to neglect communion with God is to hurt ourselves where we cannot afford it. God will respond to our efforts to know Him. The Bible tells us how; it is altogether a matter of how much determination we bring to the holy task.

One of my daughters, Emily, gave birth to a three-month-premature son named Jonathan. He weighed one pound and fourteen ounces at birth. I watched his body weight decline even though he was receiving sugar water and medication. My daughter's doctor suggested that Jonathan be fed his mother's milk in place of the sugar water. When he began to get his mother's milk, he began to grow and gain weight. This experience taught me a great lesson about spiritual growth: many Christians exist on "spiritual sugar water." Are you a Christian who is not growing because all you are being fed and are feeding yourself is "spiritual sugar water?" You can only grow as you are fed and as you feed yourself the milk and meat of your Heavenly Father, which is the Word of God.

Spiritual growth is an increasing dependence upon God. Your daily devotional life is essential to your spiritual growth as a Christian. Without it, you cannot and will not grow. But by daily spending time with God in His Word and in prayer, you will grow and mature in the likeness of the Lord Jesus Christ. II Corinthians 3:18 tells us that as we spend time in God's Word, beholding God's Son, we will experience spiritual growth. Spiritual growth is becoming like the Lord Jesus Christ.

The daily devotional life is essential to **spiritual cleansing.** The psalmist, David asked one of the most important questions recorded in the Bible in Psalm 119:9: "Wherewithal shall a young man cleanse his way?" The verse also gives us the answer, "by taking heed thereto according to Thy Word."

> *Spiritual cleansing comes in your life as you obey and personalize God's truths in your life.*

Jesus said, in John 15:3, "Now are you clean through the Word which I have spoken to you." In Ephesians 5:26, Paul states that "the church is sanctified and cleansed by the washing of the water of God's Word." I recall an experience as a young boy when my mother had instructed me to take a bath. I got in the bath tub and played in the water, not scrubbing, just washing off as the water splashed upon me. On that occasion my mother examined me after my bath and exclaimed, "All you have done is taken a spit bath, you need a thorough washing and cleansing." In reflecting on this experience, I have come to believe that too many of us as Christians only take spiritual "spit baths," and even those baths are not frequent enough. To be clean and pure as believers, we must take a daily bath in the Word of God.

The Holy Spirit gives us a vital word about cleansing in I Peter 1:22 when He says, "Seeing you have purified your souls in obeying the truth through the Spirit." Spiritual cleansing comes in your life as you obey and personalize God's truths in your life. The Holy Spirit is essential in producing spiritual cleanliness in our lives. Washing myself daily in the Word as Ephesians 5:25-26 commands has become one of the highlights of my life every day.

The words are reported to be written in the front of D.L. Moody's Bible, "This Book will keep you from sin or sin will keep you from this Book." Your daily devotional life will inspire and motivate you to be clean.

Billy Graham says that his medical missionary father-in-law, Nelson Bell, who ran a 400-bed hospital in China, made it a point "to rise every morning at four-thirty and spend two to three hours in Bible reading. He didn't use that time to read commentaries or write; he didn't do his correspondence or any of his other work. He just read the Scriptures every morning, and he was a walking Bible encyclopedia. People wondered at the holiness and the greatness in his life."

> *In my daily devotional life God has given me guidance about His will in my life.*

Your daily devotional life is essential to **spiritual guidance**. One of the great promises of God to His children is found in Psalm 32:8, which says, "I will instruct you and teach you in the way you should go; I will guide you with My eye." The psalmist David said in Psalm 119:105, "Thy Word is a lamp unto my feet, and a light unto my path." In Psalm 119:130 he said, "The entrance of Thy Word gives light." Then in Psalm 119:133, he asked the Lord "to order his steps in His Word; and not let any iniquity have dominion over him." The writer of Proverbs urges believers "to acknowledge God in all our ways and He will direct our paths" (Proverbs 3:6). John Davis, former student pastor of our church, says his devotional life is a time when he makes God the focus of his day. As we seek God's direction in our decisions through His Word and in prayer, He will give us spiritual guidance. God's Word is your spiritual road map that will give you direction and guidance in every aspect of your Christian life.

In my daily devotional life God has given me guidance about His will in my life. On one occasion when I was seeking to know God's will in regard to going to another church as pastor, the Lord gave me guidance from His Word in my daily devotional life. God used a series of verses to give me His guidance in my life.

He used Romans 8:14 which states, "For as many as are led by the Spirit of God, they are the sons of God." In this verse, God said to me that I could only go to another church if His guidance to go was as strong as His guidance that led me to my present pastorate.

In Joshua 4:10, God's Word says, "For the priests who bare the ark stood in the midst of the Jordan, until everything was finished that the Lord commanded Joshua to speak unto the people. . ." God's guidance to me in this verse was that He had not finished His work in me and through me in my present place of service.

Paul's words about Apollos in I Corinthians 16:12 gave me God's direction for my life. This verse says, "As touching our brother Apollos, I greatly desired him to come unto you with thy brethren, but his will was not at all to come at this time; but he will come when he shall have a convenient time." Paul wanted Apollos to come to Corinth just as this pulpit committee wanted me to come to their church. They encouraged me greatly, but I did not sense in my spirit that it was God's will for my life.

Paul's experience recorded in Acts 16:6-10 also gave me direction and guidance in making my decision. Acts 16:6-10 states, "Paul and his companions traveled throughout the region of Phrygia and Galatia, having been kept by the Holy Spirit from preaching the word in the province of Asia. When they came to the border of Mysia, they tried to enter Bithynia, but the Spirit of Jesus would not allow them to enter. So they passed by Mysia and went down to Troas. During the night Paul had a vision of a man of Macedonia standing and begging him, 'Come over to Macedonia and help us.' After Paul had seen the vision, we got ready at once to leave for Macedonia, concluding that God had called us to preach the gospel to them." (NIV)

In these verses the Spirit of God would not give Paul freedom to minister in Asia or Bithynia, but He did lead him to minister in Macedonia. God used these verses to guide me in not sensing freedom from the Holy Spirit to leave my present ministry, nor go to another ministry.

In Colossians 3:15, God says, "Let the peace of God rule in your hearts, to which also you are called in one body; and be ye thankful." In this verse, the Spirit of God gave me His peace about staying in my present place of service and refused to give me peace about going to another place of service.

God will give you guidance in every decision you face in your Christian life. His guidance will come to you clearly through a consistent personal devotional life.

Your daily devotional life is essential to **spiritual victory.** Psalm 119:11 says, "Thy Word have I hid in my heart, that I might not sin against Thee." God's Word hidden in the heart will give you victory over sin. Paul said to the Christians in the city of Corinth, "Now thanks be unto God, which always causes us to triumph in Christ" (II Corinthians 2:14). We are victorious in and over every circumstance in the Christian life through our personal relationship with the Lord Jesus Christ. The written Word of God points us to the life of victory through the Living Word, Jesus. Evangelist Junior Hill shared with me that his devotional life provides strength to face the challenge and burden of the day. It keeps him from losing his "God consciousness."

> *You are as safe as your personal devotions.*

John said in his first Epistle, "I have written to you, young men, because you are strong, the Word of God abides in you, and you have overcome the wicked one" (I John 2:14). The Word of God taken into your life and personalized on a daily basis will give you victory when Satan attacks you. When Satan attacked and tempted the Lord Jesus Christ, as recorded in Luke 4:1-14, Jesus defeated every assault of Satan with God's Word. Having a consistent daily devotional life will lead you to be victorious over sin, circumstances, and Satan. Andrew Murray said, "It is in the closet, in the morning watch, that our spiritual life is both tested and strengthened. There is the battlefield where it is to be decided everyday whether God is to have our all, whether our life is to be absolutely surrendered. If we gain the victory in the early morning hours, then victory during the day is sure." If you find yourself getting careless and neglecting your devotional time, confess it to the Lord and start over again. Alexander Whyte said, "The victorious Christian life, is a series of new beginnings."

The statement "You are as safe as your personal devotions" has challenged me! Intimacy with God is a lost discipline. We have adopted the theme of "have a little talk with Jesus." Our top priority should be to meet with God daily and to know Him intimately. A.W. Tozer communicates the profit of our quiet times with God in his book, *Worship and Entertainment.* "God desires to take us deeper into Himself. We will have much to learn in the school of the Spirit. He wants to lead us on in our love for Him who first loved us. He wants to cultivate within us the adoration and admiration of which He is worthy. He wants to reveal to each of us the blessed element of spiritual fascination in true worship. He wants to teach us the wonder of being filled with moral excitement in our worship, entranced with the knowledge of who God is. **He wants us to be astonished at the inconceivable elevation and magnitude and splendor of Almighty God!**" . . . "This communication, this consciousness is not an end but really an inception. There is the point of reality where we begin our fellowship and friendship and communion with God. But where we stop, no man has yet discovered, for there is in the mysterious depths of the Triune God neither limit nor end. When we come into this sweet relationship, we are beginning to learn astonished reverence, breathless adoration, awesome fascination, lofty admiration of the attributes of God and something of the breathless silence that we know when God is near."

Several years ago I faced surgery on my throat that the doctors said could be cancerous. Facing the possibility of cancer and the inability to speak, the enemy filled my life with fear. The fear had paralyzed my life spiritually and emotionally. One morning in my devotional time with the Lord He gave me II Timothy 1:7 which states, "For God has not given us the spirit of fear, but of power, and of love, and of a sound mind." I personalized this promise from God and began to live on it. It has sustained me and given me victory in my spiritual life.

Your daily devotional life is essential to **spiritual communion.** I meet many believers who admit their personal communion with God is sadly lacking and not satisfying. Their lives are full of important activities, but empty of the one thing they most desire and need: personal awareness of a living fellowship with God.

> *My devotional time with the Lord brings spiritual refreshing to my spirit,* refocuses my will and renews my mind.

The promise of God to Joshua is "As I was with Moses, so I will be with you; I will never leave you nor forsake you" (Joshua 1:5, NIV). The promise stands today for you and me. The promise is reinforced in verse 9, when He says, "Have not I commanded you? Be strong and courageous. Do not be terrified; do not be discouraged, for the Lord your God will be with you wherever you go" (NIV).

We get to know the Lord as we meet with Him in our daily devotional life. Some marriage partners spend 30 or 40 years living under the same roof, but never really get to know each other on an intimate level. Do you know the Lord on an intimate level? Ken Whitten, pastor of Idlewild Baptist Church in Tampa, Florida, says his devotional time with the Lord brings spiritual refreshing to his spirit, refocuses his will, and renews his mind.

> *The highest fulfillment of the daily devotional life is fellowship with God.*

The attitude with which you approach your daily devotional life is very important. Many Christians believe they should have a daily devotional life because they have heard teachings on its importance. Others believe it is important because great Christians have practiced a daily devotional life. Still others think it a necessary requirement for an effective Christian life. The highest fulfillment of the daily devotional life is fellowship with God. Whenever someone tells me that they don't feel very close to God, my first inquiry is, "Tell me about your personal devotional life."

Sammy Tippitt described this intimate time of communion in his book *Fire In My Bones* as follows: "The

King of kings and Lord of lords invites us to a private
meeting with Himself every day. It is an intimate meeting of a good and wonderful Father with a needy child.
In these secret meetings, we get to know the true character of the loving Father. Every day our love for Him
grows. We also receive the touch of His character on
our inner beings. We leave each meeting a little more
like the Son. We are being conformed to His image. We
seem to desire more what He desires and disdain what
He disdains."

One morning in my daily devotional time, I was reading in the fourth chapter of James. As I came to verse 8
which says, "Draw near to God, and He will draw near to
you," suddenly I was no longer just reading. It was as
though I heard the Father speak this word personally to
me. I was overwhelmed with the reality that my Heavenly Father wanted to meet with me. There was an
awesome awareness in my spirit of His presence. God
was right there with me. I could commune with Him as a
child does with his earthly father. My heart was overwhelmed with this incredible truth. I realized that
morning that because I had chosen to draw near to Him,
He was drawing near to me.

I encourage you to take time . . . make time to meet
with your Heavenly Father on a daily basis. You will
discover a depth of communion and fellowship with God
you never thought possible. Draw near to Him and He
will draw near to you.

Your daily devotional life is essential to **spiritual
health**. Paul describes the spiritually healthy Christian
in Colossians 3:15-17: "And let the peace of Christ rule
in your hearts, to the which also ye are called in one body;
and be ye thankful. Let the word of Christ dwell in you
richly in all wisdom; teaching and admonishing one
another in psalms and hymns and spiritual songs singing
with grace in your hearts to the Lord. And whatsoever
ye do in word or deed, do all in the name of the Lord
Jesus, giving thanks to God the Father by Him."

Spending time with the Lord in our daily devotional
life will vanquish fear and anxiety. The peace of God will
rule in our hearts. Your daily devotional time with the
Lord will produce spiritual balance and health in your

life. John R. Mott said, "Beginning the day with a devotional Bible study and prayer equips a believer for the day." A consistent personal devotional life will develop the mind of Christ and the outlook of Christ in your life.

In April 1963, the submarine Thresher vanished about 200 miles off the coast of New England. Apparently it had gone deeper than it was pressurized to go. In one terrifying moment, the pressure outside became greater than the pressure inside. The ocean came in like jets of steam, and 129 sailors lost their lives. When the pressure in our spiritual life from the outside becomes greater than the pressure of Christ's presence on the inside, there will be a spiritual cave in. But a daily devotional life provides a presence and health greater than the pressure of the world and of Satan.

> *A consistent devotional life will develop the mind of Christ and the outlook of Christ in your life.*

Your daily devotional life is essential to **spiritual vision**. Vision is the will, plan, purpose, and passion of God revealed by four factors: The Word of God, the Spirit of God, prayer and the needs God exposes you to. Biblical vision is the ability to see beyond the seen, the power to see with the eyes of faith something which does not exist physically or materially. Vision gives you a new freedom and a new reason to live and serve the Lord. Vision is looking at life through the eyes of God, seeing situations as He sees them. The psalmist David said, "Mine eyes are ever toward the Lord" (Psalm 25:15). Jesus said, "Blessed are the pure in heart, they shall see God" (Matthew 5:8). The Scripture says of the early disciples, "And their eyes were opened, and they recognized Him" (Luke 24:31). The writer of Proverbs said, "Where there is no vision, the people perish" (Proverbs 29:18). John Maxwell said about vision and the devotional life, "My message, my vision, my heart for the people begins with my time with God." Having a daily devotional life keeps our vision of Christ fresh, our vision of the plan of Christ foremost, and the spiritual needs of the people burning in our hearts.

Your daily devotional life is essential to **spiritual power**. The psalmist David said, "Uphold me according unto Thy Word, that I may live; and let me not be ashamed of my hope," (Psalm 119:116). The Holy Spirit gives us power to witness. This power comes as the result of a daily devotional life where the Holy Spirit fills and controls us with power from on high. We also gain power to face temptation and be victorious in our battles with sin, selfishness and Satan. My dear friend, Bobby Welch, pastor of the First Baptist Church in Daytona Beach, Florida, says his devotional life is like a soldier checking his weapons and parachute before jumping into enemy territory. Emerging from our daily devotional life, God gives us power to live the Christian life.

John Baker is a member of the church I pastor. He has served on the faculty of a Christian college. For many years he secretly and subtly became addicted to pornography. It cost him dearly. It almost cost him the loss of his wife and children. He was at the point of suicide. At the lowest point in his life he turned to God's Word. By his own testimony the reading and personalizing of God's Word rescued him from suicide, brought him home to his family, restored his relationship with Jesus, gave him victory over pornography and has made him a faithful, fruitful, and joyful Christian. There is power in the Word of God!

Your daily devotional life is essential to **spiritual consistency**. Having a definite time to meet with the Lord daily builds consistency into your Christian life. It is said of the early Christians, "They continued steadfastly in the apostles doctrine in fellowship, in prayer, and in the doctrine, breaking of bread," (Acts 2:42). If we are inconsistent in our daily devotional life it will produce inconsistency in our daily lives. Before we know it, we miss our devotional time with God, and the warmth of our relationship with God cools. Spending time every day with the Lord in His Word and in prayer will bring consistency in our Christian walk and talk.

Dr. W.A. Criswell, long time pastor of the First Baptist Church in Dallas, Texas, tells a story about an evangelist who loved to hunt. The man bought two pups that were topnotch setter bird dogs. He kept them in his large backyard, where he trained them. One morning, an ornery little vicious-looking bulldog came shuffling and snorting down the alley. He crawled under the fence into the backyard where the setters spent their days. It was easy to see he meant business. The evangelist's first impulse was to take his setters and lock them in the basement so they wouldn't tear up the little bulldog. But he decided he would just let the creature learn a lesson he would never forget. Naturally, they got into a scuffle in the backyard, and those two setters and that bulldog went round and round and round! There were growls and yipes as bulldog hair flew everywhere. The little critter finally had enough, so he squeezed under the fence and took off. All the rest of that day he whined and licked his sores. Interestingly, the next day at about the same time, here came that same ornery little bulldog . . . back under the fence and after those setters. Once again those two bird dogs beat the stuffing out of that bowlegged animal and would have chewed him up if he hadn't retreated down the alley. Would you believe, the very next day he was back, same time, same station, same results. Once again after the bulldog had had all he could take, he crawled back under the fence and found his way home to lick his wounds.

"Well," the evangelist said, "I had to leave for a revival meeting. I was gone several weeks. And when I came back, I asked my wife what had happened. She said, 'Honey, you just won't believe what has happened. Every day, at the same time every morning that little bulldog came back in the backyard and fought with our two setters. He never missed a day! And I want you to know it has come to the point that when our setters simply hear that bulldog snorting down the alley and spot him squeezing under the fence, they immediately start whining and run down into our basement. That little, old bulldog struts around our backyard now just like he owns it.'"

What the bulldog did in relation to the two setters, we need to do in our personal devotional life, stay at it. Stay with your personal devotional life with disciplined determination. When you get whipped or when you win, the secret is staying at it. Be consistent in your personal devotional life. Do it when you're up; do it when you're down. Do it when you feel like it; do it when you don't feel like it. Do it when it's cold; do it when it's hot. Keep at it! Don't give up in your personal devotional life.

PATTERNS IN THE PERSONAL
DEVOTIONAL LIFE

The success of the Billy Graham crusades is attributed to the thorough preparation of those involved in the crusades. Likewise, the success of your devotional life with God will be dependent upon your personal preparation. Making proper preparation to meet with God will cause your devotional life to be spiritually meaningful and fulfilling. Anglican Bishop Taylor Smith said, "Before I get out of bed, I look up to heaven and say, 'Lord, this bed is my altar. My body is the sacrifice. I reaffirm at the beginning of this day that I am wholly yours. Live out your life in me by the power of your Spirit.'"

Establish in your heart and mind the priority of the personal devotional life. You will always find time for what you consider to be important. There are many ways of preparing for your devotional time with the Lord. Let me offer a few suggestions that have proven helpful to me in preparing for my devotional time with Him:

— Choose a time and place for your personal devotional time with the Lord. An ideal private place may be impossible everyday; but if possible, choose a time and place where you can be alone with the Lord.

— Begin to protect your sleep time with a view to the early morning devotional time with the Lord. In other words, go to bed at a decent hour. Discipline yourself to be fresh for your devotional time with the Lord by getting adequate rest and sleep. One of the secrets to a healthy devotional life begins at night before your early morning devotional with the Lord.

— Decide on a practical means of waking up every morning. Get an alarm clock and use it. When the alarm goes off, get up and get on with your devotional time with the Lord. I have found that after consistently having my devotional time, the need for the alarm clock ceases. Isaiah 50:4 has become a reality in my life, "He awakens me morning by morning; He awakens my ear to hear like the learned."

— When you get up, do whatever it takes to get wide awake. Wash your face . . . take a shower . . . exercise . . . drink a cup of coffee or a glass of juice. Head to your meeting place with the Lord and don't get sidetracked by reading the paper, doing housework, etc. You have a divine appointment with your Lord. Don't let anything or anyone take priority over your personal time with the Lord in His Word and in prayer.

The preceding suggestions have all dealt with preparation for the devotional time. The suggestions that follow will all deal with your actual devotional time with the Lord. Let me share with you some of the ways I conduct my personal devotional time with the Lord.

The promise of God in James 4:8 is that "when we draw near to God, He will draw near to us." In this chapter, I want to share some of the ways (patterns) by which you can draw near to God in your personal devotional life. Each Christian must determine the amount of time they will give to their devotional life. Let us suppose that you choose fifteen minutes. It could be more than this, but certainly should not be less than this. This time period should serve a threefold purpose: first, for the reading of the Scriptures; second, for meditation on what has been read; and third, for worship, praise and prayer.

One of the more popular ways of conducting your devotional life begins with a brief but specific time of committing yourself to the Lord. This is followed by praying, asking the Lord to cleanse you, speak to you, change you and make you sensitive and obedient to what He says to you in His Word. This is followed by a systematic plan of reading His Word. This daily plan includes reading two chapters in the Old Testament, beginning in Genesis, a chapter in Psalms, and two chapters in the New Testament, beginning with Matthew. If you are beginning your devotional life, a good plan is to read a chapter from the Old Testament and a chapter from the New Testament. I would also suggest that you read it audibly, but softly.

While you are reading, and after you have read God's Word, take time to meditate on what God says and personalize it back to the Lord. Meditation is to reading what digestion is to eating. Just as digestion turns what we have eaten into blood, muscle, and bone, yielding energy and growth; so meditation translates what we have read into spiritual blood, muscle, and bone, yielding a life lived to the glory of God. This enables us to "grow in grace and in the knowledge of our Lord and Savior Jesus Christ" (II Peter 3:18). In another chapter we will consider the value of meditation in the personal devotional life.

The time of reading God's Word and meditating on God's Word should be followed by a time of worship, praise, and prayer. Worship is the believer's adoring response of all that he is — mind, emotions, will, and body to all that God is, says and does. It is the heart's occupation with God Himself, to the exclusion of all else. Worship and praise involves the total adoring response of man to the Eternal God. It becomes the loving ascription of praise to God. Thus with reverence, awe, amazement, and gratitude the believer is focused and occupied with God.

We should not be selfish in our praying and think only of ourselves, but also remember the needs of others.

Our praying should begin with **prayer for ourselves.** This involves the personal confession and forsaking of all known sins. Make known to your heavenly Father all your needs with the genuineness, directness and confidence of a child coming to his earthly father. Give your burdens and cares to Him. Ask for His guidance and direction. Your praying should include **intercession** for others. We should not be selfish in our praying and think only of ourselves, but also remember the needs of others. You should pray for **those in authority over you** as I Timothy 2:1,2 states, *"I exhort therefore, that, first of all, supplication, prayers, intercessions, and giving of thanks, be made for all men; for kings, and for all that are in authority; that we may lead a quiet and peaceable life in* *all godliness and honesty.* " You should pray for **laborers** in God's work as Matthew 9:36-38 states, *"But when He saw the multitudes, He was moved with compassion on them, because they fainted, and were scattered abroad, as sheep having no shepherd. Then saith He unto His disciples, 'The harvest truly is plenteous, but the laborers are few; pray ye therefore the Lord of the harvest, that He will send forth laborers unto His harvest.'"* You should pray for the **unsaved** as Romans 10:1 states, *"Brethren, my heart's desire and prayer to God for Israel is, that they might be saved."* You should pray for **those who have mistreated and despitefully used you** as Matthew 5:44 states, *"But I say unto you, love your enemies, bless them that curse you, do good to them that hate you, and pray for them which despitefully use you, and persecute you."* You should pray for **believers** as Colossians 1:9-14 states, *"For this cause we also, since the day we heard it, do not cease to pray for you, and to desire that ye might be filled with the knowledge of His will in all wisdom and spiritual understanding; that ye might walk worthy of the Lord unto all pleasing, being fruitful in every good work, increasing in the knowledge of God; strengthened with all might, according to His glorious power, unto all patience and longsuffering with joyfulness; giving thanks unto the Father, which hath made us meet to be partakers of the inheritance of the saints in light: who hath delivered us from the power of darkness, and hath translated us into the kingdom of His dear Son: in whom we have redemption through His blood, even the forgiveness of sins."* You should pray for **those who need healing** as James 5:13-16 states, *"Is any among you afflicted? Let him pray. Is any merry? Let him sing psalms. Is any sick among you? Let him call for the elders of the church; and let them pray over him, anointing him with oil in the name of the Lord: and the prayer of faith shall save the sick, and the Lord shall raise him up; and if he hath committed sins, they shall be forgiven him. Confess your faults one to another, and pray one for another, that ye may be healed. The effectual fervent prayer of a righteous man availeth much."* You should pray for **spiritual leaders** as Romans 15:30-33 states, *"Now I beseech you, brethren, for the Lord Jesus Christ's sake, and for the love of the Spirit, that ye strive together* *with me in your prayers to God for me; That I may be delivered from them that do not believe in Judea and that my service which I have for Jerusalem may be accepted of the saints; that I may come unto you with joy by the will of God, and may with you be refreshed. Now the God of peace be with you all."*

The Tabernacle Plan

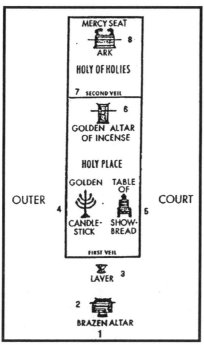

The Tabernacle plan of the personal devotional life is a method of meeting with God and experiencing God that will be a great blessing to your life. The Tabernacle God instructed Moses to build for the Israelites provides guidance and direction for getting into the presence of God in your personal devotional life.

The door (1) provides an entrance into the place where God's people could meet with Him. The doorway into God's presence is the Lord Jesus Christ. He said, "I am the door, by Me if any man enter in, he shall be saved, and shall go in and out, and find pasture" (John 10:9). When Thomas in John 14 indicated he did not know the way to God, Jesus gave eternal directions when He said, "I am the way, the truth, and the life; no man cometh unto the Father, but by me" (John 14:6).

The door to a vital personal devotional life with God is Jesus. He is our means of access to the Father. There is only one door. I begin my personal devotional time by acknowledging that the Lord Jesus is my door of access to God.

Upon entering the door, I make my way to the altar of sacrifice (2). This place of sacrifice is both a prophecy and reminder of the cross of the Lord Jesus Christ. It is a picture of the cross where Christ sacrificed Himself for me. It is an altar of thanksgiving for the sacrificial substitutionary, atoning, satisfying, all sufficient death of Christ for my sin and me. I linger here and praise God for the Lamb of God who has taken away my sin. I meditate on the cross and thank God for the blood of Jesus Christ, which cleanses me from all my sin and frees me from the punishment of sin and the bondage of sin and Satan.

The altar of sacrifice is also the place where I present myself as a living sacrifice to God on a daily basis. In the light of Jesus' sacrifice for me, I put my life on the altar of dedication and sacrifice as Romans 12:1,2 instructs me.

The next part of my daily devotional life is to come to the laver (3). The laver is the place of washing and cleansing. Here at the laver, I make confession to the One who can cleanse and forgive my sins. I claim the promise of I John 1:9, "If we confess our sins, He is faithful and just to forgive us our sins, and to cleanse us from all unrighteousness."

The priest changed his garments at the laver before entering the holy place. It was a picture of putting off his unrighteousness and putting on the righteousness of God. At this point in my personal devotional life, I frequently read and personalize the entire third chapter of Colossians. As I "put off" the things of the sinful life style and "put on" the life style of one who has been raised with Christ, the laver becomes the place where I not only confess my sins, but also the place where I confess who I am in Christ.

I move to the golden lampstand (4). The lampstand provided light in the holy place. The lampstand is a picture of Christ as the light of the world. The burning lamp requires oil. Oil is a symbol of the Holy Spirit. At this point, I ask the Holy Spirit to fill me and flow into every part of my life in order that I can worship Him, reflect Him and represent Him to those who are living in darkness.

The table of showbread is next (5). I remember that the twelve loaves of bread are a reminder of how God miraculously fed His people in their wilderness experience. The showbread is a picture of Christ, the bread of life and of the written Word of God. Here, I spend time in the Word of God listening and personalizing His Word in my life. As I feed on Christ and His Word, my life is infused with His miraculous power.

The altar of incense (6), is centered before the veil into the Holy of holies. Revelation 8:3 identifies the incense as the prayers of the saints. This is the place where I "pray about everything, by prayer and supplication with thanksgiving, making my requests known to God" (Philippians 4:6).

The veil (7) which was closed for centuries, has been torn from top to bottom, revealing the glory and splendor of God and removing every obstacle from my entering into the glorious presence of God.

I am now in the Holy of holies (8), in the presence of God. Inside the Holy of holies was the ark of the covenant containing the ten commandments, a pot of manna, and Aaron's rod. The ark of the covenant is known as the mercy seat. Blood was placed on the mercy seat by the high priest. The blood of Christ is our means of meeting God and communing with Him. The way to a personal relationship with God and intimate fellowship with Him is available to you and me. The personal devotional life is the way of daily communion and fellowship with God. The ten laws, the pot of manna, and Aaron's rod are reminders that God's Word is our authority and it must be obeyed, personalized, and applied daily.

The following is another pattern of my devotional time with God. I call it *"Beginning My Day With God."*

Beginning My Day With God

I begin by reviewing the following Scriptures:

"The Lord God has given me the tongue of disciples, that I may know how to sustain the weary one with a word. He awakens me morning by morning, He awakens my ear to listen as a disciple. The Lord God has opened my ear; and I was not disobedient, nor did I turn back."

Isaiah 50:4,5 (NAS)

"My voice shall you hear in the morning, O Lord; in the morning will I lay my request before You and wait in expectation."

Psalm 5:3 (NIV)

"And in the morning came the Word of the Lord unto me."

Ezekiel 12:8

"Blessed is the man who hears me, watching daily at my gates, waiting at the posts of my doors."

Proverbs 8:34

"Then said the Lord unto Moses, Behold, I will rain bread from heaven for you; and the people shall go out and gather a certain amount every day, that I may test them, whether they will walk in My law, or not . . . and they gathered it every morning according to their need—hunger."

Exodus 16:4,21

"For which cause we faint not; but though our outward man perish, yet the inward man is renewed day by day."

II Corinthians 4:16

After reviewing the Scriptures, I present myself to the Lord in personal worship.

> *I give myself to You Lord, not to a task or ministry,*
> *but to You alone.*

Lord, I present myself to You. Where I am is Your altar. I present (surrender, yield, give) myself to You. "I give myself to You as a sacrifice to be pleasing in your sight," *Romans 12:1*. I personally, actively, and willfully take the initiative to present myself to You. I present myself to You fully (entirely). "I yield my entire being; my spirit, soul, and body to You," *I Thessalonians 5:24*. I hold back nothing. "I am Yours and all that I have I give to You," *I Kings 20:4*. Romans 6:13 states, "Neither yield your members as instruments of unrighteousness unto sin, but yield yourselves unto God." I give You my mind, my eyes, my ears, my mouth, my heart, my will, my emotions, my hands and my feet. I give myself to You Lord, not to a task or ministry, but to You alone. I make this sacrifice by faith. It is an act of love and worship.

I often read and pray Francis Ridley Havergal's song, "Take My Life."

Take my life and let it be consecrated Lord to Thee.
Take my moments and my days, let them flow in ceaseless praise.
Take my hands and let them move at the impulse of Thy love.
Take my feet and let them be swift and beautiful for Thee.
Take my voice, and let me sing always, only, for my king.
Take my lips, and let them be filled with messages from Thee.
Take my silver and my gold; not one mite would I withhold.
Take my intellect, and use every power, as Thou shalt choose.
Take my will and make it Thine; it shall be no longer mine.
Take my heart; it is Thine own; it shall be thy royal throne.
Take my love; my Lord, I pour at Thy feet its treasure store.
Take myself, and I will be, ever, only, all for Thee.

Lord, I ask You to place Your altar fleshhooks into my body (life), so that I will not remove myself from Your altar. Crucify all the uncrucified flesh in my life. "I have no confidence in my flesh," *Philippians 3:3*. "I know that I cannot please You in the flesh," *Romans 8:8*. "Lord, by

Your Spirit, put to death the deeds and works of my flesh," *Romans 8:13.*

> *I take death now to every thing that is*
> *contrary to Your will in my life.*

Lord, I come to the altar of Calvary. I acknowledge that You died for me. "Who His own self, bore our sins in His body on the tree," *I Peter 2:24.* I also acknowledge that I died with You. "Knowing this, that our old man is crucified with Him," *Romans 6:6.* I reckon myself dead indeed to sin. I embrace the cross. "Likewise, reckon ye also yourselves to be dead indeed unto sin, but alive unto God through Jesus Christ, our Lord," *Romans 6:11.* I deny myself and I take up my cross daily, *Luke 9:23.* I take death now to everything that is contrary to Your will in my life "I die daily," *I Corinthians 15:30.* I am crucified with Christ, *Galatians 2:20.* I am dead and my life is hidden with Christ in God, *Colossians 3:3.* I will not let sin reign in my life, nor obey it through lusts, *Romans 6:12.* Sin shall not have dominion over me, *Romans 6:14.* I am now made free from sin and am a servant of God to manifest and demonstrate the fruit of holiness and everlasting life, *Romans 6:22.*

Lord, through your death at Calvary, You have spoiled (shattered, defeated) and triumphed over all the power of the enemy, *Colossians 2:14,15.* Through your death at Calvary,You destroyed (made of no effect, brought to naught) the power of the devil, *Hebrews 2:14.* Lord, you were manifested to destroy (dissolve, undo) the works of the devil, *I John 3:8.* I receive Your victory as my victory and Your life as my life.

Lord, I am alive in You, *II Corinthians 5:17,* and You are alive in me, *Colossians 1:27.* I have been raised with You, *Colossians 3:1.* Because Christ was raised from the dead, I can now walk in the newness of resurrection life, *Romans 6:4.* Lord, You have raised me up together with You and made me (enabled-privileged me) to sit with You in heavenly places in Christ, *Ephesians 2:6.* I have been raised with You, Jesus, through faith in the operation of God, *Colossians 2:12.* I have been made alive in You. You have forgiven me of all my sins, *Colossians 2:13*. Lord, You are my life, *Colossians 3:4*. You are in my life and You dwell in me by faith, *Ephesians 3:17*.

Lord, I want to know You in the power of your resurrection life, the fellowship of Your sufferings, and be made more like You in my life, *Philippians 3:10*. Make me strong in the Lord and in the power of your might, *Ephesians 3:6-10*. I know that You are able to do exceedingly abundantly above all that I can ask or think, according to Your power that is working in me, *Ephesians 3:20*.

Lord, I ask You to fill me with Your Spirit. "Be filled with the Spirit," *Ephesians 5:18*. You promised Your presence and power when the Spirit comes upon us as Acts 1:8 states, *"But ye shall receive power, after that the Holy Ghost is come upon you: and ye shall be witnesses unto Me both in Jerusalem, and in all Judea, and in Samaria, and unto the uttermost part of the earth."* You promised to supply my needs, *Philippians 4:19*, and I need desperately to be filled (controlled) by Your Spirit. Lord, You promised to pour water (Your Spirit) upon those who thirst for You and those whose lives are dry, *Isaiah 44:3; John 7:37*. Lord, I ask You to fill me with Your Spirit, *Luke 11:13; Acts 4:31*. I want You to fill me with Your Spirit in order that You may be glorified in my life, *John 7:37-39; John 16:14; Malachi 2:1,2*. I believe You to fill me with Your Spirit, *John 7:37-39*.

Lord, I put on the whole armour of God that I can stand and withstand the attacks of the enemy on my life (*Ephesians 6:11,13,14*). I put on the belt of truth. Lord, You are truth (*John 14:6*). Your Word is truth (*John 17:17*). Your truth sets me free (*John 8:32*). I love Your truth (*II Thessalonians 2:10*). I desire to walk in the truth (*II John 4; III John 4*), the truth of who I am in Christ, and in truthfulness, speaking the truth in love (*Ephesians 4:15*).

Lord, I put on the breastplate of righteousness. You are my righteousness (*I Corinthians 1:30*). I choose to live a holy, righteous life (*II Corinthians 7:1*).

I put on the sandals of the Gospel of peace. I am ready and willing to share the glorious Gospel of the Lord Jesus Christ (*Romans 1:16*). I choose to be a messenger and minister of the peace of God. You are my peace (*Ephesians*

2:14). I have peace with You through the Lord Jesus Christ *(Romans 5:1).* I choose to let the peace of God rule in my heart *(Colossians 3:15),* and keep my heart and mind *(Philippians 4:7).* I choose to fix my mind on You and let you keep me in perfect peace *(Isaiah 26:3).* I am ready to proclaim peace to all that are afar off and to those who are near *(Ephesians 2:17).*

> *I choose to live my life in a spirit*
> *and attitude of faith.*

I take the shield of faith with which I can stop all the attacks of the enemy from penetrating into my life. Lord, I choose to live by faith *(II Corinthians 5:7).* I choose to stand by faith *(II Corinthians 1:24).* I choose to live my life in a spirit and attitude of faith *(II Corinthians 4:13).* I overcome the appeal and lifestyle of the world by faith *(I John 5:4).* Lord, I choose to trust You and Your Word in every circumstance and challenge of my life *(Job 3:15).* I acknowledge that when You see me responding to the circumstances and challenges of life by faith, You intervene to accomplish Your will and purpose *(Mark 2:5).* I also acknowledge that when I act and react in faith, that it pleases You and brings glory to You *(Hebrews 11:6).*

I put on the helmet of salvation. I fill my mind with the words and promises of my Savior. His saving work and His sustaining Word remove my doubt, banish my discouragement, keep me from deception, and bring deliverance to my life *(I Thessalonians 5:8).* I cover my mind with the protective blood of Christ *(Hebrews 9:12-14).* I submit every thought and imagination to the Lordship of Christ *(II Corinthians 10:5).* I renew my mind daily by personalizing Your Word in my life *(Romans 12:2; II Corinthians 4:16).*

Lord, I take the sword of the Spirit, which is Your Word, as my defense against sin *(Psalm 119:11),* against my selfish will and desires *(Psalm 119:133),* against the attacks of Satan on my life *(Revelation 12:11).* I take Your Word as my weapon and instrument in sharing and proclaiming the good news of salvation and sanctification to those who are lost and those who are not growing in

Christ's likeness (*Hebrews 4:12*).

Lord, I choose to pray (*I Timothy 2:1,8*). I choose to pray continually (*Ephesians 6:18*). I choose to pray about every matter (*Philippians 4:6*). I choose to pray prayers of adoration, confession, thanksgiving, petition, intercession and supplication (*Ephesians 6:18*). I choose to pray in the Spirit (*Ephesians 6:18*). I choose to pray with perserverance (*Ephesians 6:18; Luke 18:1-8*). I will pray for all believers (*Ephesians 6:18; I Samuel 12:23*), and for servants of the Lord (*II Thessalonians 3:1-2*).

The Open Devotional Pattern

> *My spirit and life must be open to God*
> *and hungry for God.*

I have developed my devotional life around a method I call the open pattern. A consuming desire for fellowship with God, accompanied by a genuine openness to God, is essential to a healthy and holy devotional life. I begin my devotional time by meditating on II Corinthians 3:18, which says, "But we all, with an open face beholding as in a mirror the glory of the Lord, are changed into the same image from glory to glory, even as by the Spirit of the Lord." The thought expressed in the phrase, "an open face," implies an intimate awareness of God where there are no barriers or hardness, but an eagerness, a teachable spirit, an openness for God to say, do, lead, convict, and correct me as He pleases. My spirit and life must be open to God and hungry for God. My meditation on this verse must be accompanied by deliberately opening every area of my life to the Lord Jesus Christ. Any area of my life which is closed to Him will limit my worship of God, and will limit God's work in and through my life. The reality of my devotional life will be dependant upon my openness to the Lord. Psalm 78:41 warns us about limiting God in our lives. God says about His people, "They turned back and tempted God and limited the Holy One of Israel." Openness included instant obedience to God. A conscientious and instant choice to open my life and my spirit to God is foundational to an effective devotional life.

I ask the Lord to open my **eyes** to Him. This was Paul's prayer in Ephesians 1:18, where he prayed "that the eyes of your heart would be opened." Our spiritual eyes desperately need to be opened by the Lord and to the Lord. We need the experience of the Emmaus disciples as they walked with Jesus. The Scripture says of them, "And their eyes were opened, and they recognized Him" (Luke 24:31). David in Psalm 25:15, expressed our need when he said, "My eyes are ever toward Thee." This is also expressed in Psalm 123:1,2, which says, "Unto Thee do I lift mine eyes." Jesus said to disciples of every generation, "Blessed are the pure in heart for they shall see God" (Matthew 5:8). The Scripture records one of the spiritual secrets of Moses life when it says, "He endured as seeing Him who is invisible" (Hebrews 11:27).

Elisha's prayer for his servant (II Kings 6:17), should be our prayer everyday and in every situation. He prayed, "Lord, I pray Thee, open his eyes, that he may see." I ask the Lord to open my eyes that I may see Him and every circumstance, obstacle, opportunity that I face from His perspective.

I ask the Lord to enable me to see people as He sees them. Jesus instructs us to "lift up our eyes and look on the fields, they are white already unto harvest" (John 4:35). It is crucial that we see people as God sees them. This includes seeing our brothers and sisters in Christ as family and seeing those outside of Christ as people for whom Christ died.

Mike Otto's song expresses my heart in this matter of seeing people from God's perspective:

Let me see this world, dear Lord, as though I were looking through Your eyes.

A world of men who don't want You, Lord, but a world for which You died.

Let me kneel with You in the garden, blur my eyes with tears of agony! For if once I could see this world the way You see, I just know I'd serve You more faithfully.

Let me see this world, dear Lord, through Your eyes, when men mock Your Holy name. When they beat You and spat upon You, Lord;

*Let me love them as You loved them, just the same. Let me stand
high above my petty problems and grieve for men hell-bound eternally.
For if once I could see this world the way You see, I just know I'd
serve You more faithfully.*

Let me see this world Lord, Help me see.

Jeremiah sums up the importance of seeing God in
Lamentations 3:51, where he says, "Mine eye affecteth
my heart."

I ask the Lord daily for a heart that listens to God.

I ask the Lord to open my **ears.** David's request of the
Lord in Psalm 143:8 is also my request. He said to the
Lord, "Cause me to hear Thy loving kindness in the
morning; for in Thee do I trust. Cause me to know the
way wherein I should work; for I lift up my soul unto
Thee."

The Holy Spirit's words in Isaiah 50:4,5 have been
extremely helpful to me in preparing to hear from God.
The Scripture says, "The Lord God hath given me the
tongue of the learned (learner-disciple), that I should
know how to speak a word in season to him who is weary;
He awakens me morning by morning; He awakens my ear
to hear like a learner-disciple. The Lord God has opened
my ear, and I was not rebellious, neither turned back."

In I Kings 3:9, Solomon asked the Lord for an understanding heart. The phrase "understanding heart" means
a hearing heart . . . a heart that hears God. I ask the Lord
daily for a heart that listens to God.

In Revelation 2 and 3, the Holy Spirit urges us seven
times to "hear what He has to say to the church." I begin
my devotional time by asking the Lord to make me sensitive to His voice.

I ask the Lord to open my **heart.** The Scripture says
of Lydia, in Acts 16:14, "The Lord opened her heart." I
pray the prayer of Paul in Ephesians 1:18, "Lord, open
the eyes of my heart and flood it with Your understanding." I express the desires of my heart to the Lord, that I
will not be slow of heart to believe God and His Word
(Luke 24:25), and that my heart would burn within me

while He talks with me and while He opens the Scriptures to me (Luke 24:32). I ask the Lord every morning in my devotional time to make me a man after God's heart as David did in Acts 13:22. Only as my heart is open to Him can I become a man after God's heart.

I ask the Lord to open my **understanding.** The Scripture gives the testimony of the early disciples of Jesus in Luke 24:45, "Then opened He their understanding, that they might understand the Scripture." I ask the Lord for wisdom and discernment for my life. Spiritual understanding has come to me many times in my devotional time with the Lord. Spiritual confusion has come in my life when I have neglected my devotional time with the Lord.

I ask the Lord to open the **Scriptures** to me. Luke 24:32 says, "He opened the Scriptures to His disciples as they walked together." Words cannot adequately describe the insights, joys, and understanding of His Word that comes from the Holy Spirit when He opens and explains the Scriptures in my devotional time with Him. Time and time again, God has shown me the meaning and application of Scripture as I have waited before Him in my devotional time with God.

I ask the Lord to open doors of **opportunity** to witness, minister, and glorify Him. Paul declares that "a great door, and effectual door is opened unto me, and there are many adversaries" (I Corinthians 16:9). In II Corinthians 2:12, Paul says, "When I came to Troas to preach Christ's gospel, a door was opened unto me of the Lord." Paul asked the Colossian Christians to pray "that God would open a door of utterance for him" (Colossians 4:2,3). I pray in my devotional time that the Lord would open doors of opportunity to me and that I will walk through those doors in obedience to Him.

I ask the Lord to open my **mouth** and give me boldness to speak His truth in love. The psalmist David prayed, "Open these my lips, and my mouth shall show forth Thy praise" (Psalm 51:15). I claim the promise God gave to Moses in Exodus 4:12, "Go and I will be with your mouth and teach you what you shall say." I pray the prayer David prayed in Psalm 19:14, "Let the words of my mouth and the meditations of my heart, be acceptable in Thy sight, O Lord, my strength, and my redeemer."

The Acknowledging Plan

Let me offer another pattern that has been meaningful in my personal devotional life. I begin by acknowledging God and His presence. I have started many devotional times by simply acknowledging Him. Here is an example of acknowledging God.

Lord, I acknowledge You as:

The Living and True God . . . *"But the Lord is the true God, He is the living God, and an everlasting king: at His wrath the earth shall tremble, and the nations shall not be able to abide His indignation." Jeremiah 10:10*

The Eternal God . . . *"But now is made manifest, and by the scriptures of the prophets, according to the commandment of the everlasting God, made known to all nations for the obedience of faith." Romans 16:26*

The Creator . . . *"For by Him were all things created, that are in heaven, and that are in earth, visible and invisible, whether they be thrones, or dominions, or principalities, or powers: all things were created by Him, and for Him." Colossians 1:16*

The Unchanging God . . . *"For I am the Lord, I change not; therefore ye sons of Jacob are not consumed." Malachi 3:6*

The Holy God . . . *"And one cried unto another, and said, Holy, holy, holy, is the Lord of hosts: the whole earth is full of His glory." Isaiah 6:3*

The Sovereign God . . . *"And all the inhabitants of the earth are reputed as nothing: and He doeth according to His will in the army of heaven, and among the inhabitants of the earth: and none can stay His hand, or say unto Him, What doest Thou?" Daniel 4:35*

The Saving God . . . *"Behold, God is my salvation; I will trust, and not be afraid: for the Lord JEHOVAH is my strength and my song; He also is become my salvation."*

Isaiah 12:2

The Loving God . . . *"The Lord hath appeared of old unto me, saying, Yea, I have loved thee with an everlasting love: therefore with lovingkindness have I drawn thee."* Jeremiah 31:3

The Judging God . . . *"And to you who are troubled rest with us, when the Lord Jesus shall be revealed from heaven with His mighty angels, in flaming fire taking vengeance on them that know not God, and that obey not the gospel of our Lord Jesus Christ: who shall be punished with everlasting destruction from the presence of the Lord, and from the glory of His power."* II Thessalonians 1:7-9

The Forgiving God . . . *"Who is a God like unto Thee, that pardoneth iniquity, and passeth by the transgression of the remnant of His heritage? He retaineth not His anger for ever, because He delighteth in mercy."* Micah 7:18

The God of Peace . . . *"Now the God of peace be with you all. Amen."* Romans 15:33

The God of Wisdom . . . *"To God only wise, be glory through Jesus Christ forever. Amen."* Romans 16:27

The God of Power . . . *"Thine, O Lord, is the greatness, and the power, and the glory, and the victory, and the majesty: for all that is in the heaven and in the earth is Thine; Thine is the kingdom, O Lord, and Thou are exalted as head above all."* I Chronicles 29:11

The God of Patience . . . *"Now the God of patience and consolation grant you to be likeminded one toward another according to Christ Jesus."* Romans 15:5

The God of Hope . . . *"Now the God of hope fill you with all joy and peace in believing, that ye may abound in hope, through the power of the Holy Ghost."* Romans 15:13

The God of Grace . . . *"And God is able to make all grace abound toward you; that ye, always having all sufficiency in all things, may abound to every good work."* II Corinthians 9:8

The God of Comfort . . . *"Grace be to you and peace from God our Father, and from the Lord Jesus Christ. Blessed be God, even the Father of our Lord Jesus Christ, the Father of mercies, and the God of all comfort; who comforteth us in all our tribulation, that we may be able to comfort them which are in any trouble, by the comfort wherewith we ourselves are comforted of God."* II Corinthians 1:2-4

The God of Mercy . . . *"It is of the Lord's mercies that we are not consumed, because His compassions fail not."* Lamentations 3:22

The God of Glory . . . *"And the Word was made flesh, and dwelt among us, (and we beheld His glory, the glory as of the only begotten of the Father), full of grace and truth."* John 1:14

God my Father . . . *"To all that be in Rome, beloved of God, called to be saints: Grace to you and peace from God our Father, and the Lord Jesus Christ."* Romans 1:7

Lord, I acknowledge your presence in me:

"I am crucified with Christ: nevertheless I live; yet not I, but Christ liveth in me: and the life which I now live in the flesh I live by the faith of the Son of God, who loved me, and gave Himself for me." Galatians 2:20

Lord, I ask for your manifest presence . . . your glory in my life:

"He that hath my commandments, and keepeth them, he it is that loveth Me: and he that loveth Me shall be loved of My Father, and I will love him, and will manifest Myself to him. Jesus answered and said unto him, If a man love Me, he will keep My words: and My Father will love him, and make our abode with him." John 14:21,23

After I have acknowledged the Lord, His presence in me, and asked for His manifest presence, I **express thanks** to God. I thank Him for the personal unchanging relationship I have with Him through His Son, the Lord Jesus Christ. I thank Him for the personal fellowship I share with Him. I thank Him for daily blessings and provisions. I thank Him for the opportunities He will afford me throughout the day. I thank Him for another day of life acknowledging that "this is the day the Lord has made and I choose to rejoice in it" (Psalm 118:24). I also acknowledge "my times are in His hand" (Psalm 31:15). God has spoken to me recently in my personal devotional time with this question: "If God took everything away from you but what you have thanked Him for, what would you have left?"

> *I thank Him for the personal unchanging*
> *relationship I have with Him.*

I follow thanksgiving by presenting myself to the Lord for cleansing (Revelation 1:5,6; John 15:3; Ephesians 5:25-26; I John 1:9) . . . for worship and dedication (Romans 12:1,2) . . . to be guided and governed by His Word (Psalm 119:133) . . . to be filled with His Spirit (Ephesians 5:18; Luke 4:18-19). I then present my family, staff, and church to the Lord. I follow this by presenting my cares, concerns and burdens to the Lord (I Peter 5:7; Psalm 55:22). My next step is to listen to the Lord (Isaiah 50:4,5; Psalm 5:3).

My final step is to put on the whole armor of God (Ephesians 6:10-18). I take each piece of the believer's armor and put it on in my life for that day.

"G" Method of the Devotional Life

Another method I have used in my personal devotional life is what I call the "G" method. I use several words that begin with the letter "G" that form an eight step approach to the personal devotional life.

The first is **good** . . . The Lord is good. I begin by enumerating some of the verses and qualities of the goodness of God. Nahum 1:7: *"The Lord is good, a strong hold in the day of trouble; and He knoweth them that trust in Him."* I Chronicles 16:34: *"O give thanks unto the Lord; for He is good; for His mercy endureth for ever."* Psalm 25:8: *"Good and upright is the Lord: therefore will He teach sinners in the way."* Psalm 100:5: *"For the Lord is good; His mercy is everlasting; and His truth endureth* *to all generations.*"

The second is **give** . . . I give myself to the Lord and to others. II Corinthians 8:5: "*And this they did, not as we hoped, but first gave their own selves to the Lord, and unto us by the will of God.*" Romans 12:2: "*And be not conformed to this world; but be ye transformed by the renewing of your mind, that ye may prove what is that good, and acceptable, and perfect, will of God.*"   Luke 22:27: "*But I am among you as he that serveth.*" Galatians 5:13: "*For, brethren, ye have been called unto liberty; only use not liberty for an occasion to the flesh, but by love serve one another.*"

The third is **guide** . . . I ask the Lord to give me guidance in my day. Psalm 32:8: "*I will instruct thee and teach thee in the way which thou shalt go: I will guide thee with Mine eye.*" Psalm 27:11: "*Teach me Thy way, O Lord, and lead me in a plain path, because of mine enemies.*" Psalm 25:4,5: "*Show me Thy ways, O Lord; teach me Thy paths. Lead me in Thy truth, and teach me: for Thou art the God of my salvation; on Thee do I wait all the day.*"

The fourth is **guard** . . . I ask the Lord to guard and protect my life. Matthew 6:13: "*And lead us not into temptation, but deliver us from evil: for Thine is the kingdom, and the glory, for ever, Amen.*"   Isaiah 26:3-4: "*Thou will keep him in perfect peace, whose mind is stayed on Thee: because he trusteth in Thee. Trust ye in the Lord for ever: for in the Lord JEHOVAH is everlasting strength.*" Isaiah 59:19: "*So shall they fear the name of the Lord from the west, and His glory from the rising of the sun. When the enemy shall come in like a flood, the Spirit of the Lord shall lift up a standard against him.*" I Chronicles 4:10: "*And Jabez called on the God of Israel saying, Oh that Thou wouldest bless me indeed, and enlarge my coast, and that Thine hand might be with me, and that Thou wouldest keep me from evil, that it may not grieve me! And God granted him that which he requested.*"

The fifth is **grace** . . . I ask the Lord for grace for the day. Titus 2:11,12: "*For the grace of God that bringeth salvation hath appeared to all men, teaching us that denying ungodliness and worldly lusts, we should live*

soberly, righteously, and godly, in this present world."
II Corinthians 1:12: *"For our rejoicing is this, the
testimony of our conscience, that in simplicity and godly
sincerity, not with fleshly wisdom, but by the grace of
God, we have had our conversation in the world, and
more abundantly to you-ward."* II Corinthians 12:7-10:
*"And lest I should be exalted above measure through the
abundance of the revelations, there was given to me a
thorn in the flesh, the messenger of Satan to buffet me.
Lest I should be exalted above measure. For this thing I
besought the Lord thrice, that it might depart from me.
And he said unto me 'My grace is sufficient for thee: for
my strength is made Perfect in weakness.' Most gladly
therefore will I rather glory in my infirmities, that the
power of Christ may rest upon me. Therefore I take
pleasure in infirmities, in reproaches, in necessities, in
persecutions, in distresses for Christ's sake: for when I
am weak, then am I strong."* Hebrews 4:16: *"Let us
therefore come boldly unto the throne of grace, that we
may obtain mercy, and find grace to help in time of need."*
Romans 5:2: *"By whom also we have access by faith into
this grace where in we stand, and rejoice in hope of the
glory of God"*

The sixth is **grow** . . . I ask the Lord to grow my life
into His likeness. II Corinthians 3:18: *"But we all, with
open face beholding as in a glass the glory of the Lord,
are changed into the same image from glory to glory, even
as by the Spirit of the Lord."* II Peter 3:18: *"But grow in
grace, and in the knowledge of our Lord and Savior Jesus
Christ. To Him be glory both now and for ever."* I Peter
2:2: *"As newborn babes, desire the sincere milk of the
word, that ye may grow thereby..."* Ephesians 4:13-16:
*"Till we all come in the unity of the faith, and of the
knowledge of the Son of God, unto a perfect man, unto
the measure of the stature of the fullness of Christ: That
we henceforth be no more children, tossed to and fro, and
carried about with every wind of doctrine, by the sleight
of men, and cunning craftiness, whereby they lie in wait
to deceive; but speaking the truth in love, may grow up
into Him in all things, which is the head, even Christ:
From whom the whole body fitly joined together and
compacted by that which every joint supplieth, according
to the effectual working in the measure of every part,*

maketh increase of the body unto the edifying of itself in love." Acts 20:32: *"And now brethren, I commend you to God, and to the word of His grace, which is able to build you up, and to give you an inheritance among all them which are sanctified."*

The seventh is **go** . . . I ask the Lord to empower me and put me in situations and circumstances where I can witness and minister to others. John 20:21: *"Then said Jesus to them again, Peace be unto you: as my Father hath sent Me, even so send I you."* Matthew 28:18-20: *"And Jesus came and spake unto them, saying, All power is given unto Me in heaven and in earth. Go ye therefore, and teach all nations, baptizing them in the name of the Father, and of the Son, and of the Holy Ghost: Teaching them to observe all things whatsoever I have commanded you: and, lo, I am with you alway, even unto the end of the earth."* Matthew 20:28: *"Even as the Son of man came not to be ministered unto, but to minister, and to give His life a ransom for many."* Galatians 6:1: *"Brethren, if a man be overtaken in a fault, ye which are spiritual, restore such an one in the spirit of meekness; considering thyself, lest thou also be tempted."* Luke 22:32: *"But I have prayed for thee, that thy faith fail not: and when thou art converted, strengthen thy brethren."*

The eighth is **glorify** . . . I ask the Lord to allow me to live today to glorify Him. Jeremiah 9:23,24: *"Thus saith the Lord, let not the wise man glory in his wisdom, neither let the mighty man glory in his might, let not the rich man glory in his riches: but let him that glorieth glory in this, that he understandeth and knoweth Me, that I am the Lord which exercise lovingkindness, judgment, and righteousness, in the earth: for in these things I delight, saith the Lord."* I Corinthians 10:31: *"Whether therefore ye eat, or drink, or whatsoever ye do, do all to the glory of God."* II Thessalonians 1:12: *"That the name of our Lord Jesus Christ may be glorified in you, and ye in Him, according to the grace of our God and the Lord Jesus Christ."*

> *Three essentials to a quality personal devotional life:*
> *a quiet time, a quiet place, and a quiet spirit.*

What are the essentials of a daily devotional time?

First, you need a Bible. There are many versions and translations of the Bible. I prefer a good study Bible — don't be afraid to mark in your Bible.

Next, you need a daily devotional notebook. Keep personal notes in the notebook from your devotional time. Establish a personal devotional guide and keep it in your notebook. Record your spiritual experiences, etc. in the notebook.

You will also need a prayer list, which can also be kept in your notebook. Dr. Stephen Olford suggests the following plan. Pray every day for yourself, your family and their needs, etc. On each day of the week, pray for specific areas: Monday — missionaries and preachers, Tuesday — thanksgiving, Wednesday — workers, Thursday — tasks, Friday — families, Saturday — saints and staff, Sunday — sinners.

Along with the above-mentioned things, you will need a time and place to have your daily devotional time . . . and an expectant spirit (Mark 1:35). Byron Paulus, director of Life Action Ministries, says there are three essentials to a quality personal devotional life . . . a quiet time, a quiet place, and a quiet spirit.

What procedure should I follow in my daily devotional time?

Let me suggest the following pattern:

Decide to have a daily devotional time. Make a commitment to meet with the Lord daily. Work out the time that is best for you. If it is an initial commitment, or a renewed commitment, make it a priority commitment. Don't be discouraged by past failures.

Acknowledge the Lord's presence as your first conscious act. "Lord, You are here, and I desire to meet with

You. Speak to my heart, Lord Jesus." (Jeremiah 29:18)

Develop a plan for reading God's Word. Read the Word of God . . . personally . . . alertly . . . prayerfully . . . expectantly . . . and obediently. Read through one book of the Bible. Read the Bible as a personal letter from God.

Develop a plan for memorizing and meditating on God's Word. Meditate on what you have read. Think on it . . . think through it . . . visualize what the Scripture says.

Personalize its message in your life. Live on it. (Matthew 4:4) Obey whatever God says. Record these messages in some type of spiritual journal. Record what God says to you. Record what He leads you to do. Develop a plan for praying.

> *Share with someone else what God is doing in your life. Share it day by day.*

Let me warn you that establishing your daily devotional time will not be easy. I confess to you that it is a constant battle to maintain this time. Satan will attack you in many ways to oppose your daily devotional time. It costs . . . but it is worth whatever sacrifices it may involve. There is very little hope of living victoriously as a Christian unless you maintain your daily devotional time.

Let me encourage you to make a commitment to meet with the Lord daily and establish a meaningful devotional life. Make your personal devotional life a priority. If you have never started a personal devotional life, do so now! If you have had a personal devotional life in the past and have allowed it to be choked out so that it is not a priority, renew that commitment now! Don't be discouraged by past failure. Make your personal devotional life a continual commitment. Keep your personal devotional life fresh and daily. I love Charles Swindoll's statement "Today is the first day of the rest of your life." Start or restart your personal devotional life and don't let anything cause you to stop.

This poem by Ralph Cushman has encouraged me many times in my personal devotional time:

I met God in the morning
When my day was at its best
And His presence came like sunrise,
Like a glory in my breast.

All day long the presence lingered,
All day long, He stayed with me,
And we sailed in perfect calmness
O'er a very troubled sea.

Other lives were blown and battered,
Other lives were sore distressed,
But the winds that seemed to drive them
Bring to us a peace and rest.

Then I thought of other mornings,
With a keen remorse of mind,
When I, too, had loosed the moorings,
With the presence left behind.

So I think I know the secret,
Learned from many a troubled way:
You must seek Him in the morning,
If you want Him through the day!

OVERCOMING OBSTACLES AND FRUSTRATIONS IN YOUR PERSONAL DEVOTIONAL LIFE

There are many obstacles and frustrations you will face in starting and continuing your daily devotional life. Satan will oppose you and supply you with many reasons why you don't need to make your daily devotional life a priority. Just as Satan tempted the Lord Jesus Christ in His life and ministry, he will surely tempt you in this all-important issue of your Christian life. But in spite of the obstacles and frustrations you face in your daily devotional life, you can experience victory over every obstacle and frustration.

> *The personal devotional life is unnatural and adversarial.*

I have struggled in my devotional life because it is unnatural. The flesh opposes this activity of the spirit. Our flesh says, "no," "not now," or "not necessary" to the daily devotional life. I have struggled in my personal devotional life not only because it is unnatural, but also because it is adversarial. It is warfare. I have experienced victory in my daily devotional life when I have surrendered to the domination of the Spirit and refused the domination of the flesh.

I have experienced victory over the subtle attacks of the enemy by not giving place to him, "Neither give place to the devil" Ephesians 4:27 . . . by recognizing his strategy, "Lest Satan should get an advantage of us: for we are not ignorant of his devices" II Corinthians 2:11 . . . by submitting myself to God, "Submit yourselves therefore to God. Resist the devil, and he will flee from you" James 4:7 . . . and by resisting his attacks "Whom resist steadfast in the faith, knowing that the same afflictions are accomplished in your brethren that are in the world" I Peter 5:9.

I am being transparent as I share with you some of the specific obstacles and difficulties I have encountered in starting, developing and sustaining a vital, personal devotional life. I hope this is helpful. I also want to share how I am experiencing victory over these obstacles and difficulties.

> *Recognize the important and imperative*
> *aspect of the personal devotional life.*

Lack of discipline is an obstacle and difficulty in the daily devotional life. I have observed that many Christians are negligent and disobedient in this vital area of the Christian life. In the early years of my ministry, I preached in many churches that had Sunday School and Training Union report boards posted in their worship centers. Without failure, the lowest number on the Sunday School and Training Union boards was the number of daily Bible readers. Since I have recognized the importance of the daily devotional life and established a personal devotional life, I have asked hundreds of Christians about their personal devotional life. A large percentage of those did not have a devotional life or a consistent devotional life.

How do you overcome lack of discipline in the vital matter of your personal devotional life? You must recognize the important and imperative aspect of the personal devotional life. Joseph Parker said "If I really love my Savior, nothing will stand in my way of a personal meeting with God every morning." Oswald Chambers said, "It is impossible for a believer, no matter what his experience, to keep right with God if he will not take the trouble to spend time with God. Spend plenty of time with Him; let other things go, but don't neglect Him."

The most popular excuse for the lack of a personal devotional life is, "I just don't have time." Yet all of us are given the same number of hours each day. Each of us has 1,440 minutes to "spend" each day. We decide how to use the 86,400 seconds per day and our management of that time makes all the difference.

The Scripture poses this question, "How shall we escape if we neglect so great a salvation?" (Hebrews 2:3). I ask you to consider these questions: 1) How can you grow spiritually if you neglect your personal devotional life? 2) How can you have intimate fellowship with God if you neglect your personal devotional life? 3) How can you overcome the attacks of Satan on your life if you neglect your personal devotional life? 4) How can you serve the Lord effectively if you neglect your personal devotional life? 5) How can you worship God publicly if you neglect your personal devotional life? I urge you to take time to have a vital personal devotional life. Don't neglect it. There is an old hymn entitled "Take Time To Be Holy" that expresses the need and value of the personal devotional life.

Take Time To Be Holy
text: William D. Longstaff

Take time to be holy, Speak oft with thy Lord;
Abide in Him always, And feed on His Word.
Make Friends of God's children; Help those who are weak;
Forgetting in nothing His blessing to seek.

Take time to be holy, The world rushes on;
Much time spend in secret with Jesus alone;
By looking to Jesus, Like Him thou shalt be;
Thy friends in thy conduct His likeness shall see.

Take time to be holy, Let Him be thy guide,
And run not before Him Whatever betide;
In joy or in sorrow Still follow thy Lord,
And looking to Jesus, Still trust in His Word.

Take time to be holy, Be calm in thy soul;
Each thought and each motive Beneath His control;
Thus led by His Spirit to fountains of love,
Thou soon shalt be fitted For service above.

Once you recognize the importance of the personal devotional life, you must make the choice to discipline yourself and give priority to starting or continuing your daily devotional life. If you have the desire to have a personal devotional life and will discipline yourself, you will experience real delight in your personal devotional life.

Lack of concentration is a consistent obstacle you will face in your personal devotional life. I have found that, when my mind wanders and I have difficulty keeping my mind, heart and emotions focused on the Lord during my devotional time, several actions have helped me. Let me share with you some things that have enabled me to keep my concentration on the Lord during my quiet time.

First, when I sense a wandering of my mind and a lack of concentration of the Lord, I personalize the promises of God. I claim the promise of Proverbs 3:6, "In all thy ways, acknowledge Him." I acknowledge the Lord's presence and make Him my priority. I personalize Philippians 4:5, "The Lord is at hand." By faith, I acknowledge that the Lord is with me. I repent of my lack of concentration and concentrate on His promised presence with me.

I personalize Isaiah 26:3, "Thou wilt keep him in perfect peace whose mind is stayed on Thee, because he trusteth in Thee." I ask the Lord to give me the ability to keep my mind from wandering and to keep it stayed on Him. I verbalize the words, "Lord, I fix my heart and mind on You." I personalize II Corinthians 10:5. I ask the Lord to enable me to "bring into captivity every thought to the obedience of Christ." Claiming the promises of God and verbalizing them back to God has helped me to gain victory over lack of concentration and wandering thoughts.

Oswald Smith shares that wandering thoughts in his personal devotional life often plagued him. He got rid of the wandering thoughts by reading God's Word aloud and praying aloud. One of the many ways that Del Fehsenfeld, Jr. helped me in my Christian life is a suggestion he made about lack of concentration in his personal devotional time. When he found it difficult to concentrate and stay focused on God, His Word and will for his life, he kept a piece of paper and a pen next to him. As his mind drifted to things he needed to do that day, he would jot them down and refocus on God. At the end of his devotional time with God, he would ask God to prioritize the list and organize his schedule for the day.

Dr. Stephen Olford has helped me in my devotional life more than any other person. He advised me to communicate with the Lord when my mind and heart are wandering. He counseled me to ask the Lord these questions: "Lord, what are You saying to me? Is there a promise for me to claim? Is there an example I am to follow? Is there some sin I am to avoid? Is there a command for me to obey? Is there any new thought about God the Father, God the Son, God the Holy Spirit? Is there a new thought about Satan? Never leave a passage until you can write down what God is saying to you in order that you can pray it back to God."

> *Praise brings the manifest presence of God to us.*

Another action God has taught me when I have wandering thoughts and lack of concentration in my devotional life is to praise God. Praise brings God to us. In Psalm 22:3, the psalmist said, "But Thou art holy, O Thou who inhabitest the praise of Israel." Praise brings the manifest presence of God to us.

Praise brings us into the presence of God. In Psalm 100:4, we are encouraged to "enter His gates with thanksgiving, and into His courts with praise; be thankful unto Him, and bless His name." When you face a wandering heart and mind, make the choice to refocus on God by praising Him. Hebrews 13:15 has helped me to gain victory over lack of concentration in my devotional life. I verbalize this great verse, "By Him, therefore, let us offer the sacrifice of praise to God continually, that is, the fruit of our lips giving thanks to **His name.**"

Disruption of regular routine and interruptions are major obstacles to one's personal devotional life. This would be times such as vacations and extended periods of travel. Whatever disrupts your regular personal devotional life is an obstacle to deal with. Obviously, anything that causes you to miss a day of your personal devotional time with God is a problem. Anything that is causing me to miss several days is a major crisis. I have met this obstacle by making my personal devotional time with God the highest priority. God has helped me protect these times as if there was nothing more important. In reality, there isn't anything more important. The obstacles of disruption and interruptions can be met by a serious understanding of the vital necessity of daily meetings with God.

Another difficulty to overcome in the devotional life is getting into a "routine rut" in which your time with God slowly and gradually degenerates into a boring, non-life-changing experience. These "routine ruts" demand a fresh approach to the personal devotional life.

> *Spend a period of time fasting.*

Pam Farrell suggested some ways to wake up your quiet time in a "Discipleship Journal" article:

1. Write a letter to God about your life.
2. Write out and personalize Scripture by inserting your name into promises relevant to your life or current struggles.
3. Go on a praise walk. Thank God for everything you see.
4. Spend time singing to God. Church hymnals and books of choruses are great resources to enliven your quiet time.
5. Write down every sin that continues to haunt you. Then write I John 1:9 over each sin.
6. Read the Scripture in a posture you don't normally use.
7. Read a different translation of the Bible.
8. Praise Jesus from A to Z. For example, "Jesus, you

are amazing . . . Jesus, you are beautiful . . ." This will challenge you to think deeply about who Jesus is and why you love and serve Him.

9. Write out your prayers to Jesus.
10. Make a list of needs in your life. Find Scriptures that show how God can meet your needs. Write them next to your needs.
11. Rehearse the notes from a sermon that has blessed, challenged and changed you.
12. Read your favorite hymn. Spend some time meditating about each of the hymn's verses and its message to your life.
13. Spend a period of time fasting.
14. Have a quiet time with your wife or with one of your children.
15. Write about your relationship and fellowship with God.
16. Memorize Scripture related to your personal walk with the Lord.
17. Pray back to God some of the prayers of the Bible.
18. Utilize a daily devotional book.

Realizing that the Bible is God's personal letter to me and that prayer is personally communicating with my Lord makes my personal devotional life exciting, adventurous and fulfilling.

Another hindrance in the personal devotional life is **hurry**. Samuel Chadwick said, "Hurry is the death of prayer." It is equally the death of the personal devotional life. The "fast food" and "fast lane" lifestyle has invaded the Christian life style. People today rarely want to wait on anyone or anything.

One of the major battles you will fight in your personal devotional life is rushing into your time with God and rushing through your time with God. I have discovered that nothing is as important to my spiritual growth and welfare as my personal devotional life. Because of its importance, I cannot afford to hurry my time with God. My experience, without failure, has been that when I hurry through my personal devotional time, I miss God.

My experience has also been that when I rush through my personal devotional time, I am ill-prepared for the trials, tests, temptations, and tasks I face throughout the day. *The following poem expressed the importance of not hurrying your personal devotional time with God.*

I GOT UP EARLY ONE MORNING:

And rushed right into the day;

I had so much to accomplish

That I didn't have time to pray.

Problems just tumbled about me,

And heavier came each task.

"Why doesn't God help me?" I wondered,

He answered, "You didn't ask."

I wanted to see joy and beauty,

But the day toiled on, gray and bleak.

I wondered why God didn't show me;

He said, "But you didn't seek."

I tried to come into God's presence;

I used all the keys at the lock.

God gently and lovingly chided,

"My child, you didn't knock."

I woke up early this morning

And paused before entering the day.

I had so much to accomplish

That I had to take time to pray.

Anonymous

Several Scriptures have given me guidance in conquering the "hurry up" obstacles in my personal devotional life. Obeying the command of Isaiah 40:31 has helped me. In this passage, God promised that "They who wait upon the Lord shall renew their strength; they shall mount up with wings like eagles; they shall run, and not be weary; and they shall walk, and not faint."   —

In Psalm 46:10, God said, "Be still and know that I am God." It takes time to still your heart and mind to commune with God. I start my devotional time by saying to the Lord, "Lord, I want to meet with You. I need You. I cannot and will not face this day until I have spent time with You . . . until I get through to You . . . so, however long it takes, I am here to meet with You. Sometimes I say to the Lord, "Lord, I am here until I hear from You."

> *Seeking God is not a "hurry up" matter.*
> *It is a heart matter.*

David said in Psalm 63:1, "Early will I seek Thee . . . my soul thirsteth for Thee, my flesh longeth for Thee in a dry and thirsty land, where no water is." God speaks through Jeremiah in 29:13, "You shall seek Me and find Me when you search for Me with all your heart." These verses have helped me to realize the priority of my devotional time with God. Seeking Him is not a "hurry up" matter. It is a heart matter, and heart matters take time.

Another obstacle is **becoming discouraged through dry periods** in your walk as a believer and in your personal devotional life. I have learned that I can only have stability to the degree that my life is rooted in a daily relationship and fellowship with Christ. All of us struggle with the dry periods in our personal devotional life. I have faced those difficult dry times in a variety of ways.

Personalizing the promises of God by inserting my name has given fresh life to my personal devotional life. For example, I personalize II Timothy 1:7 in this way "God, You have not given me (Bobby) the spirit of fear, but of love, and power and a sound mind." I personalize Psalm 84:11 in this way: "No good thing will You, God, withhold from me (Bobby) when I am walking uprightly."

Another way of overcoming the dry periods is praying Psalm 139:23,24, "Search me, O God, and know my heart. Try me and know my thoughts, and see if there be any wicked way in me, and lead me in the way everlast-

ing." After I have prayed this, I write down every sin
that God reveals to me. I then confess every sin as I John
1:9 instructs me. Dealing with my sins, clears the slate
with God and gives me fresh water for my dry periods.

Read a different translation of the Bible. Reading a
new translation or comparing different ones can stimulate
new insights into Scripture. Because your eyes will not
be drawn to notes and highlighted passages from
previous study or devotional reading, the Scriptures will
feel as beautiful and inviting as a fresh snowfall on a crisp
winter morning.

Make a list of the hurts and needs in your life. As you
read God's Word and pray, write down the promises that
relate to your needs and the solutions God gives for
dealing with your hurts.

Spend a period of time fasting from food, TV, or a
hobby to spend more time with God. I will later devote
an entire chapter to the place of fasting in the personal
devotional life.

Yet another obstacle in the personal devotional life
is **not applying or personalizing God's Word to your
life.** The personal devotional life is not an end in itself.
It is meant to develop the habit of preparing to meet God
. . . of expecting to experience God . . . of concentration
on God . . . and of applying what God says to my life.

Truth is to be lived and not just learned.

It is not a matter of reading God's Word and praying
every day . . . or how much I read and how long I pray. It
is a matter of internalizing, personalizing, and applying
God's Word to my life and circumstances. Hebrews 4:2
has helped me personalize and apply God's Word to my
life. In this passage Paul said, "The Word preached did
not profit them, not being mixed with faith." Faith is a
personal and active response to the promises of God to
meet needs in my life.

Psalm 119:11 has also helped me in applying Scripture
to my life. The Psalmist said, "Thy Word have I hid in my
heart, that I might not sin against Thee." I ask God to
penetrate my mind and heart with His Word. I then ask

Him to let His Word abide in my heart. As I personalize and apply God's Word in my life, I am refreshed and live in communion with God and victory over sin, self, and Satan.

At a crucial time in my Christian life, God impressed me with this thought, "Truth is to be lived and not just learned." I heard a man of God say, "You only believe the part of God's Word that you personalize and apply to your life." Personalizing God's Word in my life has become the goal and joy of my life.

A subtle danger and obstacle in the personal devotional life is **prayerlessness**. Sometimes the prayer aspect of your personal devotional life will be omitted or given an insignificant place. Charles Finney said, "Nothing in the whole Christian religion is so difficult and rarely attained as a praying heart." An abridged prayer life is a major problem in the personal devotional life. Samuel Chadwick said, "The one concern the devil has is to keep Christians from praying. He fears nothing from prayerless studies, prayerless work, prayerless ministries. He laughs at our toil, mocks our wisdom, but trembles when we pray." One of the major strategies of Satan is to get us not to pray . . . to quit praying . . . to give less time to prayer. Graham Scroggie said, "A prayerful life is a powerful life. A prayerless life is always a powerless life." Prayerlessness is when one prays less than he ought; less than the Father desires; less than one knows he should.

Prayerlessness is a sin. I Samuel 12:23 says, "God forbid that I should sin against the Lord in ceasing to pray for you." Prayerlessness is a sin against the person of God, the plan and purpose of God, the promises of God, the power of God and the people of God.

God has taught me some life changing truths about prayerlessness in relation to my personal devotional life:

1. Prayerlessness will cause you to faint and give up in your Christian life. In Luke 18:1, Jesus said, "Men ought always to pray, and not to faint."

2. Prayerlessness will cause you to depend upon the flesh. Prayerlessness is a declaration of self-sufficiency. Jesus said, "It is the spirit that giveth life; the flesh profiteth nothing" (John 6:63). The Apostle Paul said, "Praying always with all prayer

and supplication in the Spirit" (Ephesians 6:18).

3. Prayerlessness is an open invitation to the devil . . . to deception. James said this about prayerlessness: "You do not have because you do not ask" (James 4:2 ASV). "Submit yourselves, therefore, to God. Resist the devil, and he will flee from you" (James 4:7).

4. Prayerlessness causes a loss of spiritual power. In Matthew 17:19, the disciples asked Jesus why they were powerless when facing demonic power. Jesus responded with these words, "This kind does not go out except by prayer and fasting" (Matthew 17:21 ASV).

5. Prayerlessness will cause you to lose the guidance and leadership of the Spirit. Jesus said, "When He, the Spirit of truth, is come, He will guide you into all truth" (John 16:13). Paul linked prayerlessness with quenching the Spirit in I Thessalonians 5:17 and 19 "Praying without ceasing" verse 17. . . "Quench not the Spirit" verse 19.

6. Prayerlessness leads to division and disunity among the people of God. In the Epistle of James, he instructs us to "pray one for another, that we can be healed" (James 5:16). The word "healed" includes the healing of relationships as well as healing of the body.

7. Prayerlessness brings discouragement, disappointment and defeat to your life. In Psalm 42, David ask the question twice, "Why are you cast down, O my soul?" verse 5,11. In the midst of these verses David points to the solution to being cast down when he says, "My prayer will be unto the God of my life" verse 8.

8. Prayerlessness causes fear and lack of boldness. In the early New Testament church, "When the disciples prayed, the place was shaken where they were assembled together; and they were all filled with the Holy Spirit, and they spoke the word of God with boldness" (Acts 4:31). When we do not pray we are gripped with the spirit of fear and powerlessness. Paul confirmed this truth in II Timothy 1:7 when he said, "God has not given us

the spirit of fear, but of power, and of love, and of a sound mind."

Dr. Stephen Olford gave me his formula for overcoming prayerlessness: "Pray when you feel like it. Pray when you don't feel like it. Pray till you do feel like it."

Prayerlessness must be acknowledged as a sin, confessed and forsaken. Prayer must become a vital part of your personal devotional life because it is God's way for us to know and do His will . . . because God has commanded us to pray . . . because Jesus prayed . . . because prayer is the example given to us by the early Christian church . . . because prayer is the only way we can talk to God.

Making prayer a vital part of your personal devotional life is essential. George Mueller said, "I have known my Lord for 57 years and there has never been a single day that I have failed to gain an audience with the King."

God has taught me some valuable truths about prayer that have given me direction in my personal devotional life:

1. **Talk to God as your Father** — Matthew 6:9 "our Father;" Romans 8:15 "We have not received the Spirit of bondage again to fear; but you have received the Spirit of adoption, whereby we cry Abba, Father."

2. **Talk to God as a Son** — Galatians 3:26 "For you are all the Sons of God by faith in Jesus Christ;" Galatians 4:6-7 "Because you are sons, God has sent forth the Spirit of His Son into your hearts, saying Abba, Father. Wherefore you are no more a servant, but a Son . . ."

3. **Talk to God in the Name of His Son, Jesus** — "And whatsoever ye shall ask in My name, that will I do, that the Father may be glorified in the Son. If ye shall ask any thing in My name, I will do it" John 14:13,14. "Ye have not chosen Me, but I have chosen you, and ordained you, that ye should go and bring forth fruit, and that your fruit should remain: that whatsoever ye shall ask of the Father in My name, He may give it to you" John 15:16. "Ask the Father in My name;" John 16: 23-24 "Whatever ye shall ask

the Father in My name, He will give it to you . . ."
Ephesians 2:18 "For through Him we both have
access by one Spirit unto the Father."

The name stands for the person. It speaks of His
character, qualities, position authority. . .To pray
as one with Christ. . . To declare our dependence
upon Him.

4. **Talk to God with Help from the Holy Spirit** —
Romans 8:26-27 "The Spirit helps our infirmity . . .
He makes intercession for us . . ."

5. **Talk to God with Confidence, Faith, Expectancy
and Boldness** — Hebrews 11:6 "He who comes to
God must believe that He is."

Mark 9:23 "If you can believe, all things are
possible to him that believes."

Mark 11:24 "Whatever things you desire, when
you pray, believe that you receive them, and you
shall have them."

Matthew 21:22 "And all things, whatever you
shall ask in prayer, believing, you shall receive."

James 1:5-7 . . . James 5:15 "the prayer of faith"

Hebrews 4:14-16 . . ."Let us come boldly unto
the throne of grace."

6. **Talk to God in a Spirit of Thanks and Praise** —
Psalm 100: 2-4 "Enter His gates with thanksgiving,
and into His courts with praise;" Hebrews 13:15 "By
Him, let us offer the sacrifice of praise to God
continually, that is, the fruit of our lips giving
thanks to His name."

7. **Talk to God with a Clean Life** — Proverbs 15:8
"The prayer of the upright is His delight;" Proverbs
15:29 "The Lord is far from the wicked, but He
hears the prayer of the righteous;" Psalm 4:3 "But
know that the Lord hath set apart him who is godly
for Himself; the Lord will hear when I call unto
Him."

8. **Talk to God Earnestly, Genuinely** — Hebrews 5:7
"In the days of his flesh offered up prayer and
supplications with strong crying and tears unto
Him;" James 5:16 "The effectual fervent prayer of
a righteous person accomplishes much."

9. **Talk to God Consistently and Persistently** — The secret of George Mueller's life was that he learned not only to pray but also never to give up praying. Luke 11:5-8 "persistence;" I Thessalonians 5:17 "Pray without ceasing;" Luke 18:1 "Men ought always to pray and not to faint;" Colossians 4:2 "Continue in prayer with thanksgiving." Billy Graham says, "No matter how dark and hopeless a situation might seem, never stop praying."

10. **Talk to God on the Basis of His Word and Will** — John 15:7 "If you abide in Me and My words abide in you, you shall ask what you will, and it shall be done unto you;" I John 5:14-15 "Ask according to His will"

11. **Talk to God in Order to Glorify Him** — John 14:13 "That the Father may be glorified in the Son;" I John 3:22 "And whatever we ask, we receive of Him because we keep His commandment and do those things that are pleasing in His sight." O. Hallesby said, "The fundamental law in prayer is this: Prayer is given and ordained for the purpose of glorifying God. If we make use of prayer, not to wrest from God advantages for our dear ones, or ourselves but to call down those things, which will glorify His name, then we shall see the boldest promises of the Bible about prayer fulfilled. We shall see such answers to prayer as we never thought possible."

One of the greatest teaching experiences of my life was learning to pray for God's glory. My dad was not a Christian. He worked among people who were church members but did not live as Christians. He had no confidence in Christians. I prayed earnestly that he would be saved and that my mom could have a Christian home. In my praying for my dad, I was not aware that I was praying selfishly for his salvation. While praying with a layman, Robert Dickerson, he shared with me that I was praying with a wrong motive for my dad's salvation. I will never forget his words, "Bobby, you need to pray that your dad will be saved for God's glory." As we prayed together, I asked the Lord to teach me how to pray for God's glory. I began to discover verses like John 14:13,

"Whatever you shall ask in My name, that will I do, that the Father may be glorified in the Son." I prayed two years for my dad's salvation with the express motive of his salvation being to bring glory to God. When my dad was in the hospital with heart failure, Robert Dickerson, the man who taught me to pray for God's glory, led my dad to Christ and he received a new heart for God's glory.

Kent Hughes in his book *"Discipline of a Godly Man"* makes some helpful suggestions about prayer:

Every Christian should have a prayer list, which lists, among other things, the names of his family and, if married, spouse and children. Moreover, the list ought to be detailed, featuring personal items under the names of those closest to him. I have found that small "Post-its" placed under headings help keep my list updated.

My daily prayer list carries the following headings, each with several details under it: *family, staff, secretaries and custodians, ill, grieving, important events, present problems, ministries, weekly worship, new believers, missions list.*

In addition to my daily list, I have four other lists which I try to go through once a week. List 1 has: *ongoing ill, personal requests from others, evangelism, spiritual warfare.* List 2 has: *world, USA, personal life, needed personal qualities.* List 3 has: *Christian leaders, pastors, upcoming ministries and vision.* List 4 has: *government leaders (federal, state, and local).*

Quite frankly, I could not get on at all without a prayer list, not only because it tames my wandering mind, but also because it insures that I will not neglect things that are important to me, including the many requests for personal prayer which I receive. Without a prayer list, my promises to pray for others would be totally empty. In addition, a prayer list is perfect for keeping track of answers to prayer. Dr. Sumner Wemp says, "If you want to have an effective prayer life, you must have a prayer list. A prayer list has transformed my prayer life. I easily spend one or two hours a day in prayer as a result of my prayer list. It takes me that long just to cover the lists.

Then I don't want to quit because of the joy it brings."

> *A prayer list has transformed my prayer life.*

As I reflect on my personal devotional life, the four major hindrances that I have faced are: no preparation to meet with God, no expectation from God, no concentration on God, and no application of what God says.

Praying this prayer when I am faced with obstacles and frustrations has helped me in my personal devotional life: "Almighty God, in this quiet time I seek communion with Thee. From the fret and fever of the day's business, from the world's discordant noises, from the praise and blame of men, from the confused thoughts and vain imaginations of my own heart, I now turn aside and seek the quietness of Thy presence."

Building a devotional life is like building a house. You start with the foundation and move upward. You don't expect to build a complete house on the first day. A rich devotional life doesn't happen immediately just because we want it to. Our personal devotional life will grow as we face obstacles and frustrations in the spirit of Galatians 6:9, "And let us not be weary in well doing; for in due season we shall reap if we faint not." Overcoming the obstacles to your personal devotional life will be a life changing experience. It will develop a life message in you.

FASTING AND THE PERSONAL

DEVOTIONAL LIFE

What place does fasting have in the personal devotional life? Isaiah 58 teaches that fasting is more than just abstaining from food. It is a deep, life-changing spiritual experience. Fasting is not just a mere abstaining from food for hours or days; it is a change of the heart. The ultimate purpose of fasting is to draw close to God. Thus, the practice of fasting is truly one of the keys to an awesome and intimate personal relationship with God. I have found fasting to be a vital asset to my Christian life and to my personal devotional life.

Donald Whitney in his book, Spiritual Disciplines for the Christian, writes, "Fasting is a Christian's voluntary abstinence from food for spiritual purposes." Charles Stanley says, "The purpose of fasting is to give ourselves wholly to God so He may have complete freedom with us." Tom Elliff says, "Fasting is primarily a means of heart preparation as we bow before Him. Conducted properly, fasting brings increased sensitivity to God, added time for fellowship with Him, and a heightened eagerness to cooperate with Him."

The very idea of fasting today seems strange to most twentieth century Christians. Fasting is found seventy-five times in the Bible, forty-four times in the Old Testament and thirty-one times in the New Testament. The Old Testament word for fasting means **to cover the mouth**. The New Testament word for fasting means **not to eat, to abstain from food**. Fasting is abstinence with a spiritual goal in mind. It is abstinence from anything that hinders our communion with God. Fasting is a physical expression of heart hunger for the presence of Jesus. Fasting is the expression of the soul's hunger for God . . . for fellowship . . . for intimacy. Fasting is the practice of self-denial, specifically, the abstention from food or other pleasures in order to concentrate on the spiritual. Its emphasis is not on abstention from material delights, but rather on the putting first of spiritual concerns. Fasting underlines our belief that we regard spiritual realities as more important than the physical. Fasting is a normal part of the Christian life (Matthew 6:16). Fasting is not to be done to demonstrate or display your spirituality (Matthew 6:16). Fasting is to be done unto the Father (Matthew 6:18). There is reward-value in fasting. God responds to fasting when it is done with the right purpose and motive (Matthew 6:18).

John Chrysostom, the Bishop of Constantinople in the fourth century, described fasting in this way, "Fasting is as much as lies in us, an imitation of the angels, a contempting of things present, a school of prayer, a nourishment of the soul, a bridle of the mouth, an abatement of concupiscence: it mollifies rages, it appeases anger, it calms the tempests of nature. By fasting, a man gets composed behavior, free utterance of his tongue, right apprehension of his mind."

Moses, Hannah, Samuel, Nehemiah, Esther, Ezra, David, Elijah, Daniel and many others practiced fasting in the Old Testament era. Jesus fasted (Luke 4:1-12), the church members in the New Testament fasted (Acts 13:1-4; Acts 14: 23), and Paul fasted (II Corinthians 11:27). A study of history reveals virtually every significant Christian leader fasted. Reformers including Martin Luther, John Calvin, and John Knox, and revival leaders such as Jonathan Edwards, George Whitefield, John Wesley, David Brainerd, and Charles Wesley practiced fasting as a way of life.

Jonathan Edwards fasted for twenty-two hours prior to preaching his sermon, "Sinners in the Hands of an Angry God." Billy Graham fasted and prayed during his crusade in England. During the prayer revival of 1858 in America, Christian businessmen fasted during their lunch hour and attended prayer meetings in churches near their places of work. James and Shirley Dobson, founders and leaders of the Focus on the Family ministry, fasted one day per week in behalf of their children's spiritual lives.

Fasting is supportive of the personal devotional life. The reasons or purposes for fasting are synonymous with the reasons and purposes of the personal devotional life. My reasons for fasting have been:

1. A deeper hunger for God . . . fellowship and intimacy with God. Fasting has made me more sensitive to God and desirous of a deeper fellowship with Him. Philippians 3:10 expresses my hunger, "That I may know Him, and the power of His resurrection, and the fellowship of His sufferings, being made conformable to His death."

2. A desire to be available, usable and anointed by God. My motive for fasting is to be more available to God.

3. A need for discipline in my life. The discipline of fasting associated with my personal devotional life has helped me to experience victory and consistency in weak and undisciplined areas of my life.

4. To discover the will of God in my life. As you fast and pray God will clear your understanding. His leading becomes clear and you will be able to follow God's will with complete assurance and blessing. Before I became pastor of my present church, I spent three days in fasting, praying and seeking God's direction in His Word. On several occasions over the past years, when a decision was needed about God's will, I discovered God's will during a time of fasting connected with my personal devotional life.

5. For God's intervention in circumstances, problems, and needs. When I have fasted in relation to circumstances, problems and needs, God has carried me through these experiences..He has taught me about Himself and myself..He has given me grace and guidance in every situation.

6. An understanding of Scripture. The intensity and sensitivity of my mind and will to God and His Word are increased during times of fasting associated with my personal devotional life. The Word of God becomes more personal, powerful, and precious to me.

7. Dealing with areas of temptation and sin in my life.

John Piper says fasting is meant to starve sin, not us. If there is an unresolved pocket of sin in our life, fasting in relation to the sin will break its power in your life. Fasting is not necessary every time we deal with sin, but it serves as an outward sign of genuine sorrow and grief over sin. It shows God that we are more concerned about correcting our relationship with Him, than we are about fulfilling our fleshly appetites.

8. Having a more effective prayer life. Fasting in relation to my personal devotional life has been beneficial in teaching me to wait upon the Lord, to seek Him and His will in every area and issue of my life and to continue in prayer with thanksgiving.

9. Personal spiritual examination of my life. Fasting associated with my personal devotional life has helped me to be honest and completely open in asking and allowing God to search me and show me spiritual blind spots and areas of confession and needed spiritual growth in my life.

10. Developing genuine humility in my life. Fasting has helped me deal with pride in my life. It has helped me to recognize my total dependence upon God. God has poured His grace into my life through humbling myself before Him.

11. Grace and intervention in times of sickness. For years I have fasted and prayed for my wife's healing of a muscular disease (dystonia). God has been faithful to give her grace to face extreme pain and discomfort. Recently God has seen fit to give her a greater degree of healing than she has known in years. I attribute this to God responding to the prayer and fasting of many prayer partners in our church. To Him be the glory and praise!

12. God's protection and deliverance. Every morning in my personal devotional time, throughout the day's events, and in times of fear and helplessness, as the enemy attacks my life, I cry out to Him for protection and deliverance. Fasting in relation to protection, fear and deliverance has helped me to focus on God, His promises and protection.

13. The need and necessity of revival in my life, family, church and nation. In my personal devotional time each day, I ask God to revive me, for His name's sake. I ask Him to revive my family and church. I ask Him to revive our nation and believers worldwide. Fasting in relation to revival demonstrates my hunger for God and my total dependence upon Him to manifest His person, power and glory in revival.

14. When facing crises in my life, family and church. Psalm 138:7 has sustained me and given me hope in the crises experiences of my life. I personalize the words of David, "Though I walk in the midst of trouble, Thou wilt revive me." I have claimed God's promise to revive and refresh me in the midst of troubles on a daily basis in my personal devotional life.

15. Deep concern for an unsaved or backsliding person. On numerous occasions, I have fasted and prayed for unsaved people and for believers out of God's will. I have claimed Matthew 17:14-21 in my praying for specific unsaved people and backslidden Christian. God has saved, restored and rebuilt the lives of many for whom I have fasted and prayed.

16. When there is a lack of joy in my life. When discouragement and loss of joy have plagued my life, I have fasted and prayed and claimed God's promises in Zechariah 8:19 in my personal devotional life. God has never failed to restore my joy and I have refocused on Him.

17. When God led me to fast for specific burdens, needs, and people. From time to time, God has led me to fast and pray in behalf of personal needs and burdens that my people share with me. Fasting for these needs and burdens has become an essential part of my ministry as a pastor and as a caring Christian.

Fasting is supportive of the personal devotional life.

I have followed the following guidelines that have made fasting a vital part of my personal devotional life:

1. God initiates the fast.
2. The fast must be combined with Scripture reading, meditation and personalizing Scripture.
3. The fast must be combined with prayer.
4. The fast must focus on some spiritual purpose.
5. Fast secretly and God will reward openly.
6. Don't fast to achieve selfish purposes.
7. Don't fast to impress others with your spirituality.
8. Don't fast to attempt to force God's hand.
9. Don't fast as a substitute for repentance and godly living.

The benefits of fasting in relation to your personal devotional life are enumerated in Isaiah 58. They are:

1. God will set you free from sin and its bondage in your life. This freedom includes cleansing and deliverance from besetting sins (Isaiah 58:6).
2. God will set you free from heavy burdens (Isaiah 58:6).
3. God will set you free from oppression (Isaiah 58:6).
4. God will direct you to give and minister to the poor and hungry (Isaiah 58:7,10).
5. God will turn your heart to your own family and their needs (Isaiah 58:7).
6. God will give you spiritual insight and discernment (Isaiah 58:8).
7. God will bring healing to you (Isaiah 58:8).
8. God will give guidance in right living (Isaiah 58:9).
9. God will provide and protect you in your life (Isaiah 58:8).
10. God will answer your prayer (Isaiah 58:9).
11. God will heal your accusative spirit (Isaiah 58:9).

12. God will silence you from unwholesome and untruthful speech (Isaiah 58:9).

13. God will guide you continually (Isaiah 58:11).

14. God will meet your needs (Isaiah 58:11).

15. God will give you strength to do His will and work (Isaiah 58:11).

16. God will make you fruitful and refreshing (Isaiah 58:11).

17. God will make you a rebuilder and restorer (Isaiah 58:12).

18. God will cause you to delight in Him (Isaiah 58:13,14).

19. God will exalt you (Isaiah 58:14).

20. God will fulfill His purposes and promises in your life (Isaiah 58:14).

I have found it profitable to set aside one day a week for prayer and fasting. I have integrated this day with my personal devotional life. I have also found it helpful to set aside several days of fasting, prayer and devotional reading of God's Word to get God's guidance in my life, family and church. My wife and I have practiced fasting together for family needs, health needs, and our personal spiritual needs.

Lorne Sanny, of the Navigators ministry, has some helpful suggestions about spending a day in prayer. Why spend a day in prayer? Perhaps you haven't spent a protracted time in prayer because you haven't recognized the need for it. Maybe you aren't sure what you would do with a whole day on your hands, *just to pray.* Why take this time from a busy life? What is it for?

1. **For extended fellowship with God** — beyond your morning devotions. It means just plain being with and thinking about God. God has called us into the fellowship of His Son, Jesus Christ (I Corinthians 1:9). Like many personal relationships, this fellowship is nurtured by spending time together. God takes special note of times when His people reverence Him and think upon His Name (Malachi 3:16).

2. **For renewed perspective.** Like flying over the

battlefield in a reconnaissance plane, a day of prayer gives opportunity to think of the world from God's point of view. Especially when going through some difficulty we need this perspective to sharpen our vision of the unseen, and to let the immediate, tangible things drop into proper place. Our spiritual defenses are strengthened while "we fix our eyes not on what is seen, but on what is unseen. For . . . what is unseen is eternal" (II Corinthians 4:18).

3. **For catching up on intercession.** There are nonChristian friends and relatives to bring before the Lord, missionaries on various fields, our pastors, our neighbors and Christian associates, our government leaders — to name a few. Influencing people and changing events through prayer is well known among Christians, but it is too little practiced. As times become more serious around us, we need to reconsider the value of personal prayer, both to accomplish and to deter.

4. **For prayerful consideration of our own lives before the Lord** — personal inventory and evaluation. You will want to take a day of prayer on a periodic basis, and especially when facing important decisions. On such a day you can evaluate where you are in relation to your goals and get direction from the Lord through His Word. Promises are there for you and me, just as they have been for Hudson Taylor, George Mueller or Dawson Trotman. It is in our times alone with God that He gives inner assurance of His promises to us.

5. **For adequate preparation.** Nehemiah, after spending "certain days" seeking the Lord in prayer, was called in before the king. "Then the king said unto me, 'For what dost thou make request?' So I prayed to the God of heaven. And I said unto the king, 'If it please the king. . .'" — and he outlined his plan (Nehemiah 2:4,5). Then Nehemiah said, "I arose in the night, I and some few men with me; neither told I any man what my God had put in my heart to do at Jerusalem" (2:12). When did God put

in his heart this plan? I believe it was when he fasted and prayed and waited on God. Then when the day came for action, he was ready.

I heard a boy ask a pilot if it didn't take quick thinking to land his plane when something went wrong. The pilot answered that no, he knew at all times where he would put down if something went wrong. He had already planned that out ahead of time.

So it should be in our Christian life. If God has given us plans and purposes in those times alone, we will be ready when opportunity comes to move right into it. We won't have to say, "I'm not prepared." The reason many Christians are dead to opportunity is not because they are not mentally alert, but they are simply unprepared in heart. Preparation is made when we get alone with God.

God wants you to have a dynamic personal devotional life. If God leads you to fast in connection with your personal devotional life fasting will do for you what it has done for others, what it has done for me.

Fasting is personal. It has helped me in seeking God and knowing His purpose and power in my life. It has enabled me to know His presence and peace in a greater way. It has enriched my personal devotional life. It has given me an opportunity to please God and trust God with circumstances, problems and needs. I recommend God directed fasting as a vital part of your personal devotional life. It will bring an incredible consciousness of God and contentment in God.

MEDITATION AND THE

PERSONAL DEVOTIONAL LIFE

Meditating on God's Word is a practice that is both commanded and commended by God to His children. God's command to Joshua is His command to us. This command states, "This Book of the law shall not depart from your mouth, but you shall meditate on it day and night, so that you may be careful to do according to all that is written in it; for then you will make your way prosperous, and then you will have success" (Joshua 1:8, NAS).

Another passage that indicates the importance of meditation is Psalm 1:2,3. The psalmist writes that the blessed person "delights in the law of the Lord, and in His law he meditates day and night . . . And in whatever he does, he prospers" (NAS).

> *Meditation is concentrating on God's truth.*

Meditate means to muse, to mull over, to think about it with the mind, to examine it. To meditate on God's Word is to tune our spirits to God's Word. It is visualizing what God's Word says to us. J. I. Packer has defined meditation "as the activity of calling to mind, and thinking over, and dwelling on, and applying to oneself, the various things that one knows about the works and ways and purposes and promises of God." Meditation is thinking on the Scriptures and on the greatness and grace of God, His ways, His attitudes, and His principles.

Charles Stanley in a messaged entitled, "Life's Most Important Activity" said this: "Meditation is concentrating on God's truth, mulling over what God says by integrating it into your mind, will and emotions. Meditation is absorbing God's Word into your mind. It is allowing the living and powerful Word of God to penetrate your will and emotions, putting God's truth into your inner-most being. Meditation is absorbing and thinking on the person and work of Jesus Christ. Meditation is gleaning spiritually, threshing through the counsel of God for words spoken directly to your heart, mind and spirit."

Bill Gothard has given some great and timely insight into the nature of meditation.

What is Meditation?

Meditation is a pleasant "murmuring" of Scripture to yourself. Psalm 1:2 ". . . In his law doth he meditate. . ."

Meditation is a quiet reflection upon the words of Scripture. Psalm 119:99: ". . . Thy testimonies are my meditation."

Meditation is a musical repetition of God's Word. Psalm 19:14: "Let the words of my mouth and the meditation of my heart . . ."

Meditation is a prayerful reviewing of Scripture. I Timothy 4:15: "Meditate upon these things . . ."

Meditation is a communing with God in the language of His own written Word. Psalm 119:48: ". . .Thy commandments, which I have loved; and I will meditate in thy statutes." Meditation is "talking to the King in the King's own words."

Meditation is building your day and night around Scripture. Psalm 119:97: "O how love I Thy law! It is my meditation all the day." Job 23:12: ". . . I have esteemed the words of His mouth more than my necessary food."

Meditation is worshipping God is spirit and in truth. John 4:24: "God is a Spirit: and they that worship Him must worship Him in spirit and in truth." Psalm 104:34: "My meditation of Him shall be sweet. . ."

The relationship of meditation to the personal devotional life is foundational and life changing. Meditating on God's Word affects every area of life. It causes our spirits to be quieted. It brings a peace that surpasses all understanding. It enables you to sit before the Lord and enjoy His peace in any and every circumstance.

It sharpens our perception and understanding of God's Word. The words of Scripture are living words. Meditating on God's Word enables us to discover the rich wealth and personal application of His Word to our lives.

Meditation purifies our souls. As you read and apply God's Word to your life it has a cleansing effect. Meditation on God's Word makes cleansing a continual process in the life of the Christian. It also motivates us to be consecrated to Him and His ways.

Meditation clarifies and solidifies God's direction in our lives. The more we think on God's Word and ways, the more we are influenced to know and follow God's direction. Meditating on God's Word brings either confirmation or caution about our decisions and directions.

Meditating on God's Word builds an awareness of who we are in Christ. Knowing who we are in Christ enables us to live by faith and not by feelings and circumstances. It gives us surety, strength and stability in an unsure world.

Meditation increases and enlarges the boundaries of our faith. As we meditate on God's Word our faith grows from "little faith" (Matthew 8:26), to "strong faith" (Romans 4:20). Meditation builds us up in our most holy faith (Jude 20).

Meditation enlarges our view of God and develops a more personal intimacy with God. The Bible is a revelation of God's heart. As you meditate on it, you become a person after God's heart. Meditation also deepens our hunger for God. The more of God's Word we internalize in our lives, the more our hunger for God increases.

Meditation is the key to successful Christian living. Psalm 1:2,3 and Joshua 1:8 promise success and prosperity to all who meditate on the Scriptures day and night. The purpose of meditation is to build Scripture into your life so that it becomes a very vital part of your thinking, your character, and your behavior. This goal is achieved through the following four steps.

1. **Memorization:** Select an appropriate passage of Scripture and begin your week by attempting to memorize it word for word. Write the verse on a 3 x 5 card, and carry it with you. Refer to it often.

2. **Harmonization:** During the day, list the areas of your life that are being brought into harmony with the basic truth of the Scripture.

3. **Personalize:** Change the Scripture passage to the first person . . . as if you were speaking the passage from your own personal experience. Example: John 3:16, *"For God so loved me that He gave His only begotten Son that I might believe on Him and I will not perish, but I will have eternal life."*

4. **Verbalize:** By the end of the day you can verbalize the passage to God in the form of a prayer. Do this each morning, throughout the day and each night.

Meditation is the key to successful Christian living.

The most profitable and enjoyable time of any day is that time invested in personal meditation of God's Word. It directs our path for the day.

I close this chapter with a testimony from a great man of prayer and faith who practiced meditation daily. George Mueller (1805-1898) is famous for establishing orphanages in England, for being a man of prayer, and for joyfully depending on God for all his needs. How did he kindle this joy and faith? In 1841 he made a life-changing discovery. His testimony from his autobiography emphasizes the supreme importance of meditation in the Christian life.

"While I was staying at Nailsworth, it pleased the Lord to teach me a truth, irrespective of human instrumentality, as far as I know, the benefit of which I have not lost, though now . . . more than forty years have since passed away.

"I saw more clearly than ever, that the first great and primary business to which I ought to attend every day was, to have my soul happy in the Lord. The first thing to be concerned about was not, how much I might serve the Lord, how I might glorify the Lord; but how I might get my soul into a happy state, and how my inner man might be nourished. For I might seek to set the truth before the converted, I might seek to benefit believers, I might seek to relieve the distressed, I might in other ways seek to behave myself as it becomes a child of God in this world; and yet, not being happy in the Lord, and not being nourished and strengthened in my inner man day by day, all this might not be attended to in a right spirit.

"Before this time my practice had been, at least for ten years previously, as an habitual thing, to give myself to prayer, after having dressed in the morning. Now I saw, that the most important thing I had to do was to give myself to the reading of the Word of God and to meditation on it, that thus my heart might be comforted, encouraged, warned, reproved, instructed; and that thus, whilst meditating, my heart might be brought into experimental communion with the Lord. I began therefore, to meditate on the New Testament, from the beginning, early in the morning.

"The first thing I did, after having asked in a few words the Lord's blessing upon His precious Word, was to begin to meditate on the Word of God; searching, as it were, into every verse, to get blessing out of it; not for the sake of the public ministry of the Word; not for the sake of preaching on what I had meditated upon; but for the sake of obtaining food for my own soul. The result I have found to be almost invariably this, that after a very few minutes my soul has been led to confession, or to thanksgiving, or to intercession, or to supplication; so that though I did not, as it were, give myself to prayer, but to meditation, yet it turned almost immediately more or less into prayer.

"When thus I have been for awhile making confession, or intercession, or supplication, or have given thanks, I go on to the next words or verse, turning all, as I go on, into prayer for myself or others, as the Word may lead to it; but still continually keeping before me, that food for my own soul is the object of my meditation, and that my inner man almost invariably is even sensibly nourished and strengthened and that by breakfast time, with rare exceptions, I am in a peaceful if not happy state of heart. Thus also the Lord is pleased to communicate unto me that which, very soon after, I have found to become food for other believers, though it was not for the sake of the public ministry of the Word that I gave myself to meditation, but for the profit of my own inner man.

"The difference between my former practice and my present one is this. Formerly, when I rose, I began to pray as soon as possible, and generally spend all my time till breakfast in prayer, or almost all the time. At all events I almost invariably began with prayer . . . But what was the result? I often spent a quarter of an hour, or half an hour, or even an hour on my knees, before being conscious to myself of having derived comfort, encouragement, humbling of soul, etc.; and often after having suffered much from wandering of mind for the first ten minutes, or a quarter of an hour, or even half an hour, I only then began really to pray.

"I scarcely ever suffer now in this way. For my heart being nourished by the truth, being brought into experimental fellowship with God, I speak to my Father, and to my Friend (vile though I am, and unworthy of it!) about the things that He has brought before me in His precious Word.

"It often now astonishes me that I did not sooner see this. In no book did I ever read about it. No public ministry ever brought the matter before me. No private interaction with a brother stirred me up to this matter. And yet now, since God has taught me this point, it is as plain to me as anything that the first thing the child of God has to do morning-by-morning is to obtain food for his inner man.

"As the outward man is not fit for work for any length of time, except we take food, and as this is one of the first things we do in the morning, so it should be with the inner man. We should take food for that, as every one must allow. Now what is the food for the inner man: not prayer, but the Word of God: and here again not the simple reading of the Word of God, so that it only passes through our minds, just as water runs through a pipe, but considering what we read, pondering over it, and applying it to our hearts. . .

> *The fruit of meditation is a lifestyle of praise.*

"I dwell so particularly on this point because of the immense spiritual profit and refreshment I am conscious of having derived from it myself, and I affectionately and solemnly beseech all my fellow-believers to ponder this matter. By the blessing of God I ascribe to this mode the help and strength which I have had from God to pass in peace through deeper trials in various ways that I had never had before; and after having now above forty years tried this way, I can most fully, in the fear of God, commend it. How different when the soul is refreshed and made happy early in the morning, from what it is when, without spiritual preparation, the service, the trials and the temptations of the day come upon one!"

The fruit of meditation is a lifestyle of praise. You discover the majesty of God and His concern over even the little details of your life. This leads to an increasing awareness of His presence in your normal routine and this leads to a lifestyle of praise and thanksgiving. You actually see God at work in your life, family, church and vocation.

Meditation must be a priority. Like Bible reading and prayer, meditation cannot be fully beneficial unless done regularly. It is not something we do occasionally. It must be a consistent part of your personal devotional life. It will change your life!

PERSONAL DEVOTIONAL LIFE
AND JOURNALING

One of the first instructions God gave Moses after the Exodus was to "write these things in a book." Recalling the mighty acts of God was an essential element in reminding the people of God's goodness, greatness and power. An invaluable tool for the preservation of God's work in your life and the application of His truth in our lives is a personal devotional journal.

My own use of a personal devotional journal began by keeping a notebook of insights gleaned from my personal Bible study. I treasure those moments of God-given insight and illumination. Over a period of time, I began to include prayer requests, answers to prayer, promises, problems, needs, hopes and plans for the future.

The Puritans were noted for their mastery of Bible study and meditation, and their success was largely attributed to the use of a personal diary. As everyone must one day give an account of himself to God, the Puritans likewise believed that a Christian should give a daily account of his life. This was best accomplished in a personal diary. By recording their spiritual times with God, they grew closer to God.

Throughout history, great Christian leaders have kept personal devotional journals as an aid to their spiritual life and growth. These leaders used their journals to record God-given insights and expressions of their personal struggles. Such men included George Washington, Charles Spurgeon, John Bunyan, John and Charles Wesley, David Brainard, David Livingston, and Jim Elliot.

> *Journaling is recording your daily walk with God.*

These Christians, although extraordinary in their achievements, used a tool so simple that it can work for anyone. An ordinary notebook may seem insignificant, but when used as a spiritual diary, it can greatly benefit your personal devotional life.

In a sense, large sections of the Bible itself could qualify as journals. The book of Job is written in the style of a journal, telling the story of one man's suffering and his encounter with his "comforting" friends. Ecclesiastes is another kind of journal, which records Solomon's attempt to find meaning in life apart from God. The four gospels are written accounts of the life and ministry of Christ. The Book of Acts is a journal that records the life of the early church.

Journaling is recording your daily walk with God. It may include a list of prayers that have been asked of and answered by God. Sometimes it involves interaction with God in Scripture. It can be one of the best methods of charting your spiritual growth. More than anything, the practice of journaling reminds me that my walk with God is a daily experience that can be chronicled and measured. A personal devotional journal is a book in which you keep a personal record of events in your life, of your different relationships, of your response to things, of your feelings about things, of your search to find out who you are in Christ and where you are in your spiritual pilgrimage.

Donald Whitney's definition of journaling is very helpful. "A journal . . . is a book in which a person writes down various things. As a Christian, your journal is a place to record the works and ways of God in your life. Your journal also can include an account of daily events, a diary of personal relationships, a notebook of insights into Scripture, and a list of prayer requests. It is where spontaneous devotional thoughts or lengthy theological musings can be preserved. A journal is one of the best places for charting your progress in the other spiritual disciplines and for holding yourself accountable to your goals."

There are many benefits in keeping a personal devotional journal. Let me share with you some of the benefits, with the hope that it will inspire and motivate you to start or continue your personal devotional life. Journaling will help you to see the Christian life as a daily experience of worship, adoration, fellowship, intercession, discipleship, witness and ministry. It will help you to be consistent in your Christian life. It will bring spiritual balance to your Christian life.

• Journaling will help you to personalize God's Word in your life. In my journaling, I include two issues on a daily basis: 1) What God is saying to me. 2) What I am saying to God.

• Journaling is a source of encouragement and inspiration. It causes me to be aware of God's working in my life on a daily basis. It encourages me to remember the faithfulness of God in every circumstance of my life. It gives me hope for the present and the future.

• Keeping a daily personal devotional journal is a constant reminder of how God has met my needs, and that He is able to supply all my needs through His riches in Christ Jesus (Philippians 4:19).

• Journaling helps to grow us into spiritual maturity. As we reflect on our spiritual pilgrimage, we gain spiritual understanding of the dynamics of the Christian life, the obstacles, the doubts, the crises and temptations, and the means of grace to overcome these. Daily journaling is a constant reminder that God wants to renew us in our inner man day by day (II Corinthians 4:16).

• Journaling helps to clarify our priorities. The experience of Jesus with Martha and Mary recorded in Luke 10:38-42 is an eternal reminder that the one thing above all other things in the Christian life is sitting at Jesus feet, hearing His Word. This is the personal devotional life, and keeping a written record of what He says to you will help you to keep your priorities in line.

> *Journaling helps you to be more accountable to God and to others.*

• Keeping a personal journal will give you guidance and direction in making decisions and overcoming difficult situations in your Christian life. Writing things down crystallizes issues and problems. When we record our fears and anxious moments, we can later see how great a God we have. Somehow, in writing out those fears and needs in our journal, their power over us diminishes and God's direction becomes clear.

• Journaling helps to be more accountable to God and to others. One of the greatest needs in the Christian life and in Christian leaders is accountability. As we discipline ourselves in our daily devotional life and record our daily activities, it will motivate us to be more accountable. As we discipline ourselves to what the Puritans referred to as "the self-watch journal," we constantly reset our course to walk in the way of Christ.

• Journaling also leads to authenticity and honesty. Writing in my journal helps me to be truthful. It makes it easier for me to face the truth about myself. It forces me to respond to life circumstances honestly. Reading the Psalms has helped me to see how honest, open and authentic David was about his life. Recording my dealings with God and others does the same for me. It will do the same for you also!

• Journaling will cause one to be more sensitive to God and to the needs and hurts of others. As God ministers to you in your personal devotional life, you will become more aware of His presence and purpose. This leads to an empathy and care for others. Documenting these things in your journal will be a constant reminder of your need of God and the needs that others have in their lives.

• Journaling leads to freshness in the Christian life. One of the master strategies of the enemy is to cause you to be passive and stagnant in your Christian life. Journaling will help you to stay fresh and active in your walk, work and witness for the Lord.

• Journaling will help you to reflect and learn from your experiences in life. If you keep a record of God's dealings with you, it will encourage and inspire you to trust Him in difficult times. Writing down what God is doing and what you are experiencing will spur you on to greater faith and trust in Him. John Wesley recorded nightly in his journal the sins he had committed, the places he had preached, the people he ministered to and discipled, the truths God had taught him that day and the people and issues for which he had prayed.

Since I established my personal devotional time as a priority, I have kept a personal devotional journal. I treasure the truths God has revealed to me. Years of journaling demonstrate the providence and goodness of God in my life. The record of many answered prayers builds my faith and proves that God answers prayers. Journaling increases the power, effectiveness and urgency of your prayer life. One of the ways God has blessed and enriched my prayer life is by praying for specific people and needs on different days of the week.

On Mondays, I pray for missionaries, ministers, meetings, morality, maturity, and messages. Tuesdays, I give thanks for blessings, provisions, and answered prayers. I also pray for those in places of authority. I pray in relation to trust, togetherness, and my temple. On Wednesdays, I pray about worship, workers, witnessing, my walk as a believer, weariness, wisdom and warfare. On Thursdays, I pray for tasks, troubles, my time, tests, temptations and I pray through the Ten Commandments. On Fridays, I pray for families, financial needs, fellowship, fire and fervency, freshness, furtherance of the gospel and fulfilling the Great Commandment and Great Commission. On Saturdays, I pray for souls, services, sensitivity, speech, stability, and a servant spirit. On Sundays, I pray for the sick, saints, suffering, those going through storms, for submission and for God's supernatural power in our services.

• Journaling will make you aware of spiritual blind spots in your life. As you journal and review your journaling, the Spirit of God will show you areas of neglect and need in your life.

• Journaling will cause you to be open and aware to how God is using the lives of others to teach and transform you. I frequently write down what God is teaching me through the lives of those with whom He brings me in contact.

> *Journaling will make you aware of*
> *spiritual blindspots in your life.*

Many people recognize the value of journaling and begin with good intentions, but within a month or two they find they have abandoned this discipline. Keeping a spiritual journal can quickly become another duty for which there is limited time. In his leader's guide to the popular discipleship course, *Experiencing God,* Claude King lists ten questions designed to help people recognize God's work in their lives. If you have difficulty finding things to record in your journal, you may wish to use this list to guide you as you write.

1. What has God revealed to you about Himself?
2. What has God revealed to you about His purposes?
3. What has God revealed to you about His ways?
4. What has God done in your life or through your life that has caused you to experience His presence?
5. What Scripture has God used to speak to you about Himself, His purposes or His ways?
6. What particular person or concern has God given you a burden to pray for? What has He guided you to pray for in this situation?
7. What has God done through circumstances that have given you a sense of His timing or direction concerning any aspect of His will?
8. What word of guidance or truth do you sense God has spoken to you through another believer?
9. What adjustment is God leading you to make in your life?
10. What acts of obedience have you accomplished this week? What further steps of obedience do you

know God wants you to take?

Not everyone who keeps a journal makes daily entries. Your schedule may cause you to miss a day or two each week. Occasionally, you may find yourself making both morning and evening entries in your journal. Don't quit in frustration if you miss a day. Begin again the next day and keep writing. Just as you stumbled the first few times you began walking, so you may experience ups and downs as you develop the discipline of journaling. Developing a personal devotional journal has become one of the greatest sources of motivation and inspiration in my life. I recommend it. It has changed my life. It will change your life.

THE BENEFITS AND BLESSINGS

OF THE PERSONAL

DEVOTIONAL LIFE

I recently saw a sign that said, "Christian education doesn't cost, it pays!" As I reflected on the meaning of the sign, I thought about the personal devotional life. It does cost, but oh how it pays. The blessings and benefits of the personal devotional life are worth every bit of the cost, discipline and sacrifice involved in having a vital personal devotional life.

As I enumerate the blessings and benefits of the personal devotional life, I warn you that there must be decision, discipline, and devotion to this most important aspect of the Christian life. Remember, you must be a "doer of the Word and not only a hearer" (James 1:22). The words of Jesus in John 13:17 are so applicable to the personal devotional life: "If you know these things, happy are you if you do them."

David Williams has written a song that describes the benefits and blessings of the personal devotional life:

In The Morning
In the morning, that's when I meet my Savior
And then, I His wondrous presence know.
In the morning, I tell Him all my problems,
That's when I to God's own throne room go.

In the morning He shows me all His mercies,
And forgives my sins from day to day.
In the morning He understands my heartaches,
As I seek to walk with Him each day.

In the morning He fills my cup with blessings,
And His love melts all my fears away.
In the morning we walk and talk together
As He listens to all that I say.

In the morning I sing to Him His praises
That have caused this sad heart now to sing.
In the morning my heart is broken often
As I think how few lost souls I bring.

In the morning I hear him whisper gently
That in time He'll show me all His will.
In the morning, that's when He shows me simply
How 'that day' His will I can fulfill.

In the morning I bring my friends and loved ones,
And each need I always leave Him there.
In the morning He answers through the Bible
As I spend this time with Him in prayer.

In the morning He opens wide my vision
Of a world that's dying now in sin.
In the morning He makes me want to tell them
How that they can have real peace in Him.

> *A daily personal devotional life*
> *will establish you in God's will.*

One of the greatest benefits of the personal devotional life is that it guides and establishes your life in the will and ways of God. David asked the Lord in prayer to "establish his word in his life" (Psalm 119:38). Filling your life with the Word of God will establish and fortify your life, marriage, family and church. A daily personal devotional life will establish you in God's will, and everyday will be a day of godly fulfillment in your life. You will be able to face the storms of life and the subtle attacks of Satan. Your personal devotional life will secure you in every aspect of your Christian life.

The personal devotional life will cleanse you from sin and fortify your life against sin. David said in Psalm 119:11, "Thy word have I hid in my heart, that I might not sin against Thee." Jesus said in John 15:3, "You are clean through the Word I have spoke to you." Paul said, "That we experience sanctification and cleansing with the washing of water by the Word" (Ephesians 5:25). David said in Psalm 119:133, "Order my steps in Thy Word, and don't let any iniquity have dominion over me." My daily devotional life in the early morning hours has been my spiritual shower to prepare me for the day. It serves to keep me clean spiritually; it strengthens me in the temptations I face, and enables me to stand against the attacks of the enemy on my life.

The personal devotional life gives me God's perspective for the day. It trains my mind to think on God and His ways. It enables me to see people, problems, potentials, and circumstances through the eyes of God. It will refine your spiritual perception. You will get discernment in God's Word and ways. I pray daily the prayer of David, "Lord, give me understanding according to Thy Word," Psalm 119:169. God's Word will give you His counsel. "God's testimonies also are my delight and my counselors" (Psalm 119:24). You will see God as He really is. You will see your circumstances in the light of who God is and who you are in Christ. You will see your past, present, and future from God's perspective. You will see yourself as God sees you.

> The personal devotional life leads to
> a state of peace in situations we face.

The personal devotional life will supply you with God's provision for the pressures you face and the needs you have. Psalm 119:50 has sustained me many times with these words: "This is my comfort in my affliction; for Thy Word has given me life." Pastor E.F. Hallock gave wonderful counsel when he said, "I have lived my Christian life and served my Lord by living on the promises of God."

My daily devotional life has been the greatest means of God showing Himself strong in my weakness and need. Day after day God has met me at the point of my need in His Word.

The personal devotional life leads to a state of peace in situations we face. God's promise in Psalm 119:165, "Great peace have they that love Thy law," continually gives me peace in the midst of every situation. As you sit before the Lord in your devotional time, His peace will control your heart and life. God's Word personalized in your life will change you physically, psychologically, socially, emotionally, mentally and spiritually. "The peace of God, which passes all understanding will guard and keep your heart and mind through Christ Jesus" (Philippians 4:7). Jesus said, "Peace I leave with you, My peace give I unto you, not as the world gives, give I unto you. Let not your heart be troubled, neither let it be afraid" (John 14:27). This peace becomes operative in our lives as we feed on the Word of God in our daily devotional lives. Jesus said, "These things have I spoken to you, that in Me you might have peace" (John 16:33). We can have God's peace through the Word of God. No one has expressed this like Isaiah. He said, "Thou will keep him in perfect peace, whose mind is stayed on Thee: because he trusteth in Thee," Isaiah 26:3.

The personal devotional life will develop your faith as a believer. "Faith comes by hearing the Word of God" (Romans 10:17). One of the best ways to develop and strengthen your faith is to spend time in the Word of God. The more of God's Word you take into your life and the more consistent you are in your personal devotional life, the more your faith will grow and develop. One of the weakest areas in the lives of many Christians is living by faith. Because of this I have sought God for ways to grow and develop my faith. In my personal devotional life, God has shown me in the Scripture how to develop my faith.

1. **By feeding on God's Word.** Your faith will grow to the degree you feed yourself the Word of God on a daily basis. Paul says in Acts 20:32 that "the word of God's grace will build you up."

2. **By exercising the faith you have.** As long as your faith is active it will be growing. When your faith

becomes passive your faith life will decrease. Every time you face a challenge, command, crises or circumstance with confidence in God and commitment to God your faith will grow.

3. **By the testing and trying of your faith.** Genesis 22 is the classic experience of faith being tested. The Scripture says, "God did test Abraham," Genesis 22:1. The ageless question is "Why does God test my faith?" God has shown me through Abraham's experience that He has divine purposes in testing our faith. They are:

1) To prove the genuineness of it.

2) To grow us in His likeness.

3) To expand and enlarge our ministry.

4) To use our testimony.

5) To deepen our communion with God and our love for God.

6) To prove Himself to us.

4. **By living in the light of Jesus' return.** The words of Jude 21, "Looking for the mercy of our Lord Jesus Christ unto eternal life," encourage us to live by faith.

5. **By living for the redemption and restoration of others.** Expressing compassion and care for others as expressed in Jude 22,23 will develop and expand your faith.

6. **By living a life of thanksgiving, worship, and praise.** Colossians 2:7 teaches that as you abound in thanksgiving your faith will be strengthened.

7. **By praying for an increase in faith.** According to Luke 17:5, the apostles requested Jesus to increase their faith. Prayer is an expression of faith that enables your faith to grow stronger.

8. **By forsaking sin and worldliness.** The faith of Moses grew as he refused to identify with the worldly lifestyle of Egypt (Hebrews 11:24); as he chose to suffer with the people of God rather than enjoy the pleasures of sin for a season (Hebrews 11:25).

9. **By living under the lordship of Christ.** Colossians

2:5,6 teaches that our faith will be settled and strong as we live daily in the lordship of Christ.

10. **By choosing to please and glorify God.** Hebrews 11:6 teaches that as we choose to please and glorify God our faith grows strong.

The personal devotional life aids in personal intimacy with God. Meeting God daily in His Word and in prayer develops a close and intimate relationship with God. God speaks to us in the Scripture. As we sit before the Lord and listen to His Word, He becomes more real and intimate to us. This is demonstrated in Mary's listening to the words of Jesus in Luke 10:38-42. Time and time again as I have met with the Lord in my personal devotional life, God has refreshed me, revealed Himself to me and brought personal revival to my life. If you desire to be close to God, you need to recognize that you are reading a personal letter from God in the Bible and talking with God personally in prayer creates intimacy with Him. My co-laborer in ministry, Paul Young, says that through his quiet times he has learned to be in "awe" of God. By being in awe of God, he has learned to love the things God loves and hate the things He hates.

Paul also shared with me that one of the greatest benefits of the personal devotional life is the security that it has given his children through the years. He shares it this way: "During the formative years of my children's lives, we lived in a home that had all the bedrooms upstairs, and we had a living room and a dining room downstairs. Like most homes in those days our living room was seldom used. I did, however, have a comfortable chair where I had my quiet time each morning. That chair was positioned just below the stairs, and little did I know the impact of the position of that chair. One of my most treasured possessions is a book that my daughter Kim gave me. It is a book compiled and edited by Gloria Gaither called 'What My Parents Did Right.' In the front of the book Kim wrote these words:

"This book would not be complete without giving honor to my dad and the things he has done right . . . My dad is a man of prayer. Each morning as I came downstairs for breakfast, I'd find him in his easy chair with his Bible open, spending time alone with God. During my teenage years, he took the time to pray with me before school each week. What a profound impact it had on my life to hear my dad weep over our family, our friends and our church. When asked how it is possible that all three of us girls managed to escape the rebellion and peer pressure of adolescence, all I can do is point to God's promise in James 5:16 that '. . . the effectual fervent prayer of a righteous man availeth much.'"

> *One of the greatest benefits of the personal devotional life is experiencing God's guidance in your life.*

The personal devotional life has enabled me to know God's power in my life. Many times I have prayed the prayer that David prayed in Psalm 119:28, "Strengthen me according unto thy Word." In times of weakness God has shown Himself strong to me and in my behalf as I have yielded to Him in my personal devotional life. I have claimed II Corinthians 12:7-10 on many occasions, "And lest I should be exalted above measure through the abundance of the revelations, there was given to me a thorn in the flesh, the messenger of Satan to buffet me, lest I should be exalted above measure. For this thing I besought the Lord thrice that it might depart from me. And he said unto me, *My grace is sufficient for thee: for My strength is made perfect in weakness.* Most gladly therefore will I rather glory in my infirmities, that the power of Christ may rest upon me. Therefore I take pleasure in infirmities, in reproaches, in necessities, in persecutions, in distresses for Christ's stake: for when I am weak, then am I strong." As I have prayed about witnessing to unsaved people, He has given me power to witness. According to His promise in Acts 1:8, "Ye shall receive power after the Holy Spirit is come upon you, and you shall be My witnesses." As I have prayed over opportunities and obligations of serving the Lord, He has given me power to serve Him effectively. Depending totally upon His promise in Colossians 1:29, "I have labored (served) according to His working, which is at work in me mightly." As I have faced temptations in my daily life, God has given me power to resist and flee them as promised in I Corinthians 10:13, "There hath no temptation taken you but such as is common to man: but God is faithful, who will not suffer you to be tempted above that you are able; but will with the temptation also make a way to escape, that ye may be able to bear it." God has also given me power to become, to be and to do what He commands and desires in my life. This power comes from spending time with the Lord in your personal devotional life.

One of the greatest benefits of the personal devotional life is experiencing God's guidance in your life. David's prayer in Psalm 32:8 is my prayer during times of seeking God's guidance in my life. The promise of God is "I will instruct you and teach you in the way which you shall go; I will guide you with Mine eye." Many minor and major decisions in my life have been made in my personal devotional times with the Lord. God has been faithful to give me guidance and direction in my life, family, and ministry.

The personal devotional life has been the means of experiencing God's hope and comfort in my life: God's promises have turned my fear and despair into hope on numerous occasions as I have claimed these promises from His Word in my personal devotional time, "Remember the word unto thy servant, upon which thou hast caused me to hope," (Psalm 119:49). "They that fear Thee will be glad when they see me; because I have hoped in Thy word," (Psalm 119:74). "My soul fainteth for Thy salvation: but I hope in Thy word," (Psalm 119:81). "Unhold me according unto Thy word, that I may live: and let me not be ashamed of my hope," (Psalm 119:116). "I prevented the dawning of the morning, and cried: I hoped in Thy word," (Psalm 119:147). Many mornings, my discouragement has been replaced with God's comfort as I spend time with Him in my personal devotional life. These verses have brought God's incredible comfort to my life: "This is my comfort in my affliction: for Thy word hath quickened me. The proud have had me greatly in derision: yet have I not declined from Thy law. I remembered thy judgments of old, O Lord; and have comforted myself,"

(Psalm 119:67). "Before I was afflicted I went astray: but now have I kept Thy word," (Psalm 119:50-52). "It is good for me that I have been afflicted; that I might learn Thy statutes," (Psalm 119:71). "I know, O Lord, that Thy judgments are right, and that Thou in faithfulness hast afflicted me," (Psalm 119:75). "Unless Thy law had been my delights, I should then have perished in mine affliction," (Psalm 119:92). "I am afflicted very much: quicken me, O Lord, according unto Thy word," (Psalm 119:107). "Consider mine affliction, and deliver me: for I do not forget Thy law," (Psalm 119:153). This process is beyond human explanation but it is very definitely a benefit and blessing. My personal devotional life has been the arena where potential panic was turned into praise. The encouragement, which comes from daily times with the Lord, is one of the greatest blessings of the Christian life. Personal devotional times are truly times of refreshing from the presence of the Lord.

The personal devotional life is a daily opportunity to pray, to commune with God, to confess sin, to adore the Lord, to express thanks and praise, to petition, to intercede, and to worship and wait before the Lord. My personal devotional life has been the greatest time to develop an effective and growing prayer life. Psalm 119:169-170 has given me guidance and growth in my prayer life, "Let my cry come near before Thee, O Lord: give me understanding according to Thy word. Let my supplication come before Thee: deliver me according to Thy word."

> *The most important activity in the life of any Christian is their personal devotional life.*

My personal devotional times with God have pointed out areas of pride, falsehood, and spiritual blindness in my life. God has shown me subtle areas of pride in my life. His Word accompanied by His Spirit has shown me areas of unreality and lack of integrity. God has revealed to me areas of spiritual bondage in my life in personal times with Him that have not been revealed at other times. The failure to have a personal devotional life is one of the greatest areas of bondage to many Christians. A godly Christian couple involved in intercession shared with me that 90% of the problems Christian people face could and would be solved if they had a personal devotional life. If you have never started the daily practice of a personal devotional life, I hope you will make the choice to start today. If at some time in your life you have started a devotional life, but have stopped or haven't been consistent, I hope you will choose to begin again like Jonah when God gave him a second chance. If you are involved in a daily personal devotional life, don't ever let anything or anyone divert you from this most important aspect of the Christian life.

The most important activity in the life of any Christian is their personal devotional life. Everything in your Christian life rises or falls on your personal devotional life. Here are several quotes some great Christians said about their personal devotional life:

"If I could live my life over again, I would be more consistent in my own devotional life. I would give at least one hour a day to prayer and devotional reading of the Bible." *Roy Fish*

"If I could live my life over again, I would pray more. I would develop a more intimate devotional life." *W. Herschel Ford*

"If I could live my life over again, I would study the biographies of great spiritual giants and learn how to have a deeper and more meaningful devotional life." *David Grant*

"If I could live my life over again, I would have a quiet time everyday and study the Bible for my own spiritual enrichment." *Homer Lindsey Sr.*

"I've been a Christian 51 years, and it's the cultivation of my relationship with the Lord that has brought me to a point of wanting, desiring, and needing His refreshing every day." *Thelma Wells*

"My devotional time in the morning is my personal time with the Father. Consistent intake of the Word of God and consistent prayer time form the basis of my fellowship with the Father." *Jerry Brooks*

"It's very important to spend time in the Word everyday. I don't think it is possible to live in the power of the Holy Spirit without feasting on God's Word daily." *Bill Bright*

"Meaningful, leisurely quiet times with the Lord are the main source of my daily relationship with God. Dependence on the Holy Spirit is my first priority, and my quiet times flow out of that." *Anne Ortuland*

"The whole purpose of our devotional life is to develop intimacy with God. To keep a sense of intimacy with God, you need to spend time with Him." *Vonette Bright*

"I have found there are three essential conditions for a successful devotional life: a quiet time, a quiet place, and a quiet heart." *Byron Paulus*

"Over the years, I have come to see that devotions are not so much an obligation of the Christian life, as it is an incredible opportunity to know the God of the universe. He has issued to you and me an invitation to draw near to Him, to walk right into the Holy of Holies, to enter into an intimate love relationship with Him. Devotions have become for me, not so much a duty (although there are still days when it is just that), as a delight-an awesome privilege to share sweet union and communion with the Bridegroom of my soul." *Nancy Leigh DeMoss*

"Without exception, the men and women I have known who make the most rapid, consistent, and evident growth in Christlikeness have been those who develop a daily time of being alone with God for Bible intake, prayer, and private worship." *Donald Whitney*

"I've come to believe that of all the things we can teach our children, nothing could be more profitable in equipping them for life — whatever or wherever it sends them — than a commitment to meditate daily on God's Word." *Tim Grissom*

The personal devotional life is life changing not only to pastors, missionaries, etc., but also to Christian lay people. Consider the testimonies of lay people in my church who have chosen to make their personal devotional life a priority:

"Making the personal devotional life an essential part of my life has caused me to walk closer to the Lord and live daily for Him."

"My personal devotional life has caused me to confess my sins instantly, to be more sensitive to the Holy Spirit's presence and leading, and has developed in me a deeper love for Christ, for Christians and non Christians."

"My personal devotional life connects me to the Father."

"I have seen many answers to prayer. My faith in God has been strengthened. I have an increased burden to intercede for others."

"I personally would be in a great big mess, not to mention how I would have my wife and children involved in a mess. I went seventeen years as a Christian without having a personal devotional life. My life was a mess. God used my personal devotional life to transform my mind, my life, my marriage, and my children."

"Because of starting a personal devotional life, I understand the personal nature of God's Word. I am gaining victory over my temper. My love for the Lord and others is increasing. My love for God's Word is also increasing."

"Through my personal devotional life God is teaching me and encouraging me in the difficult times in my life. He is teaching me to obey Him and His Word."

"In my personal and private times with God, He brings peace to my heart, guidance to my life, wisdom in my decisions and hope for the future."

"God has blessed me in my personal devotional life through answering my prayers, through revealing Himself to me in His Word, and through showing me who I am in Christ."

"The biggest blessing is that I have never been more

at peace than I am since I committed myself to have a daily personal devotional life and this peace is growing continually."

"I am finding God's guidance and help with my daily problems."

"The greatest blessing of my personal devotional life is that if I feel no one else wants to listen or cares, I know the Lord is listening and that He cares for me."

"The personal devotional life has brought me closer to the Lord. I am enjoying an intimacy with Him that I did not know was possible."

"Because of my personal devotional life, I am closer to the Lord and others. I am not fearful now. I trust His Word more."

"Starting and continuing my personal devotional life has developed faithfulness and consistency in my life."

"My personal devotional time with the Lord in the mornings is my appointment with God to be filled with His Spirit."

"My personal devotional life is where God has taught me how to worship and praise Him."

"God is nurturing me spiritually in my personal life. I thank God that I am beginning to grow as a Christian. I believe my spiritual growth is because of my personal devotional life."

"I have learned to feed myself spiritually and I have learned to pray in my personal devotional times."

"Maintaining my personal devotional life in the Word and prayer has kept me from sin."

"My fellowship with God and with other believers has been enriched through my personal devotional life."

"My personal devotional life is the greatest source of my accountability to God, to my family and to my church."

As I bring to a close this work on the personal devotional life, I want you to be challenged by the words of

Chuck Swindoll who said, "Today is the first day of the rest of your life." Today, you can begin your personal devotional life! Today, you can reestablish your personal devotional life! Today, you can continue your personal devotional life! Today, and everyday, make your personal devotional life a priority! It will be a life changing experience.